D0921024

THE
CHASAM SOFER

The Story of
Rabbi Moshe Sofer

by
Yaakov Dovid Shulman

CIS PUBLISHERS
New York · London · Jerusalem

Published and distributed
in the U.S., Canada and overseas by
C.I.S. Publishers and Distributors
180 Park Avenue, Lakewood, New Jersey 08701
(908) 905-3000 Fax: (908) 367-6666

Distributed in Israel by
C.I.S. International (Israel)
Rechov Mishkalov 18
Har Nof, Jerusalem
Tel: 02-518-935

Distributed in the U.K. and Europe by
C.I.S. International (U.K.)
89 Craven Park Road
London N15 6AH, England
Tel: 81-809-3723

Cover credits: Deenee Cohen
Typography: Nechamie Miller

Cover illustration reproduced
from a Tiefenbrun original

ISBN 1-56062-117-6 hardcover
1-56062-118-4 softcover

PRINTED IN THE UNITED STATES OF AMERICA

Dedicated to the memory of
my Uncle Chaskiel, of blessed memory,
whom I had hoped to have pleased
with its publication.

Table of Contents

Introduction

RABBI MOSHE SOFER, THE CHASAM SOFER, WAS BORN INTO TUMULTU-
ous times. He grew up in Germany in the latter half of the
eighteenth century, at a time when the Vilna Gaon was still the
shining light of Lithuania Jewry and when the second generation of *Chassidus* was attracting hundreds of thousands of
Jews.

In Frankfurt, the young Moshe Sofer studied with two
great Talmudic scholars and masters of *Kabbalah*, Rabbi
Nassan Adler and Rabbi Pinchas Horowitz.

At the same time, another man was also alive who typified
a different direction in which Jews were moving. This was
Moses Mendelssohn, the father of the *Haskalah* movement,
which many Jews used as a path to leave Judaism, and which
was a precursor of the Reform movement.

There was another man alive at this time, a non-Jew, who

also had a profound effect on all European Jews. This was Napoleon Bonaparte. His bid for power and his political agenda symbolized the change in European thought at the time and the beginning of the struggle for political freedom. But the promise of political emancipation for the Jews brought with it danger as well, for the gentile emancipators expected the Jews to abandon Torah and assimilate into European Christian society.

At the beginning of the nineteenth century, the Chasam Sofer was thrust against his will into communal service. Starting out as rabbi of the small town of Dresnitz, he advanced to the prestigious community of Mattersdorf and eventually became Rav of Pressburg (today Bratislava) and effectively leader of Hungarian Jewry, one of the most powerful rabbinic leaders in Europe. He had wanted nothing else than to remain within the four cubits of Torah learning so that he might dedicate his life to serving G-d. He was outstanding in all areas of Torah learning, in both its revealed and hidden aspects. In addition, his character was impeccable. He was a *gaon* and a *tzaddik*. But he felt that G-d wanted him to leave "the tent of Jacob" and go to battle against "the hands of Esav."

The Chasam Sofer spent the next thirty-three years as the spiritual guide of Pressburg. Politically, the Jews of Hungary swung back and forth between emancipation and repression, as the influence of Napoleon overcame Hungary and then was beaten back. At the same time, the Haskalah and Reform movements were making strong efforts to change Jewish society from the inside and to force change by using government pressure.

The Chasam Sofer became the foremost representative of Orthodox Jewry in the fight against assimilation and Reform. He went further than retaining the status quo in Pressburg—he strengthened the position of the Orthodox rabbis. Taking a strong and unwavering stand, he made Pressburg a largely impregnable fortress against the anti-Torah spirit of the age. When he passed away, his position was passed on to his son. Thus, Orthodox Jewry was fortified in Pressburg for generations to come.

The Chasam Sofer presented to the outside world the face of a political and organizational leader. But he was also a great Torah leader. The Chasam Sofer began a *yeshivah* that taught five hundred students, the largest *yeshivah* since Babylonian times. He wrote voluminous novellae (*chiddushim*) on Talmud and on the *Chumash*. Most of all, perhaps, he issued many letters, his responsa (*sheilos uteshuvos*), not only to questioners in Hungary but all over Europe, as well as from far-off places such as the Land of Israel.

When the Chasam Sofer stepped out of the role of independent student of Torah and into the role of Torah leader, he did not miss a step. He was unwaveringly assured, composed and unerring. His era demanded a leader who could rule with rigor. The Chasam Sofer filled the role so well that this appeared to be his natural character.

In reality, the Chasam Sofer was by nature a warm-hearted, loving person. But when faced with the challenge of serving G-d by taking on a new, strict persona, the Chasam Sofer did not hesitate. Perhaps he could be compared in this to Avraham Avinu, whose test was also to conquer his great warm-heartedness and serve G-d with an aspect alien to him, the aspect of strictness.

The Chasam Sofer was both a deep thinker and a man of action. He succeeded in all the areas in which he served. The spirit of loyalty to Torah that he and his children instilled in Hungarian Jewry has lasted for a hundred and fifty years, surviving the anti-Torah movement of Reform, as well as the anti-Torah aspects of various other cultural and political movements, and surviving the gentile prosecution that culminated in the Holocaust.

13

His influence has been very important and he still commands great respect and allegiance. This narrative shall attempt to do justice to his achievements, with G-d's help, and to present an accurate description of his life, based on reliable sources.

The main source used for this book was the *Chut Hameshulash*, written by the Chasam Sofer's grandson Rabbi Shlomo Sofer, with much consultation with the Chasam Sofer's children; it is an excellent source on the subjects and reflects accuracy in reportage and faithfulness to the teachings of its subject. Other works consulted were *Minhagei Baal Hachasam Sofer*, and *Hachasam Sofer* by Eliezer Katz, *The Hatam Sofer: His Life and Times* by Rabbi Moses J. Burak and *Pressburg Under Siege*, translated from the Chasam Sofer's diary by Rabbi Avraham Yaakov Finkel.

This work aims to present an anecdotal biography of the Chasam Sofer, one which stresses incidents in the Chasam Sofer's life, yet also alludes to the political and social background of his time. Episodes have been fleshed out for the sake of immediacy. However, no incidents or characters have been invented.

Y.D.S.
5 *Adar Sheni*, 5752

1

The Birth of a Leader

THE SUN HUNG OVER THE TREES, LARGE AND PENDULOUS, SINKING into the lap of the western evening. The deepening sky was bringing with its flush of indigo the *Shabbos* that the Jews had longed for the entire week.

In the synagogue, a building crushed between teetering, wooden buildings that leaned upon one another on the narrow, streets of the Jews' Quarter, the *minyan* had finished chanting the six Psalms to greet the *Shabbos* Queen. It was the custom in Frankfurt-am-Main to bring in the *Shabbos* early. The golden rays of the setting sun streaked across the walls of the synagogue, across the faces of the Torah scholars and the merchants, the simple Jews and the learned Jews, who stood ready to sing and welcome the *Shabbos* Queen. The voice of the cantor was sweet, and the dust motes in the lemon rays of sunshine that coursed through the synagogue floated and danced freely, as though even they were dancing to welcome the *Shabbos* Queen.

"*Lechah Dodi*," the cantor began to sing. The old, wooden floor-boards creaked beneath his feet, as though they too, the very floor of the synagogue, wished to join the welcome of the *Shabbos*.

The men chanted the resonant, evocative words of longing and welcome: "Come, my Beloved, to greet the bride, let us greet the *Shabbos*!"

Verse by verse, the cantor greeted the mystic presence of the spirit of *Shabbos Kodesh*, and all the men chanted together with him. "Let us go out to greet the *Shabbos*, the source of blessings . . . Rise up, royal city, the holy place of the King . . . Awake, awake, for your light has come, arise and shine, awake, awake, sing forth . . ."

The very benches in the little synagogue, the very walls suffused with the golden-lemon streams of sunlight, the voices of the men, the *aron kodesh* glowing deeply in the setting sunlight, the faces of the men, grew impassioned and exalted. Now the *Shabbos* was coming. Now G-d's presence would no longer be concealed by the folds of the workaday week. Now they would come again to the island of the World-to-Come where they could take refuge from the exile. "Your enemy will be destroyed and all your troubles will be removed; your G-d will rejoice over you like a bridegroom rejoicing over his bride." The men stood up to turn and greet the *Shabbos* presence entering the synagogue. They stood up to turn to the back of the *shul*, to the west from which the spirit of the *Shabbos* Queen would come, wing over them and rest upon them with a sudden, quiet spirit of intimate and wordless, other-Worldly joy.

The men turned around, many of them outstanding Torah scholars, for Frankfurt-am-Main was a major center of Torah learning. At his seat by the eastern wall stood Rabbi Avraham

Abush, Chief Rabbi of Frankfurt-am-Main. Not far from him was Rabbi Shmuel Sofer, a well-known Torah scholar and scribe.

The singing grew louder: "Come, my Beloved, to meet the bride . . ." The longing for the comfort of *Shabbos* was almost tangible.

But Rabbi Sofer's mind was divided. Part of him floated with the melody of the haunting tune that welcomed in the yearned-for *Shabbos*. But another part of him was in anxiety, still on edge. He wished to hurry home to his wife, to find out what the news was, to learn of good news with relief.

For ten years, he and his wife Reizl, who was thirty-six years old, had been childless. The previous *Yom Kippur* they had been visited by a holy man named Rabbi Zeligman, a man who sat and learned Torah his entire life, wearing *tefillin* and wrapped in a *tallis*, a man who had emulated Ben Azzai, the *Tanna* who had not married. Rabbi Zeligman had promised them that they would soon have a child.

Now, on the seventh of *Tishrei*, 5523 (1762), Reizl Sofer had been in labor for some time. Rabbi Sofer's thoughts flickered from the sweetness of the incoming *Shabbos* to thoughts of his wife at home with the midwife. How was it? What would happen? Would everyone be all right?

The words, "Come in peace, crown of her Husband," were about to spring to the cantor's lips. Suddenly, the synagogue door that they were facing was flung open.

"Rabbi Abush! Wait!" a young man cried out breathlessly, his face red and sweating.

The cantor and the congregation were abruptly halted. Their faces turned as one to Rabbi Abush.

"What is wrong?" Rabbi Abush asked.

"I beg your pardon," the young man spoke choppily, catching his breath. "I was sent by Mrs. Reizl Sofer. She is still in labor and she would like the congregation not to take on

17

Shabbos yet. She is afraid that if she gives birth when Frankfurt-am-Main has already taken on the *Shabbos*, she would be the cause of the breaking of *Shabbos*."

Rabbi Abush stood a moment, considering. A spirit seemed to pass over his face. "Very well," he said authoritatively. "It is right to wait. She will give birth to a boy whose teachings will illumine the eyes of Torah scholars and whose prayers will save the Jews." Rabbi Abush turned his glance toward Rabbi Sofer. "He will be called Moshe."

"What is he saying?" murmured one of the men. "Does he have *ruach hakodesh*?"

Rabbi Abush said nothing more. He turned and sat down at his seat and opened a *Gemara*.

The confused and interrupted men took his example and also sat down at their seats and began learning and speaking with one another.

The sun sank slowly, disappearing below the trees and buildings, and drawing with it the entire curtain of the Friday sky into the lap of the cobalt blue horizon of the soothing *Shabbos*.

The child who was born that late afternoon to Rabbi Shmuel and Reizl Sofer was Moshe Sofer. He would grow up to be the chief rabbi of Pressburg and one of the greatest Torah figures of his time. In his life, turmoil would roil the Jewish world. The inner life of Rabbi Moshe Sofer would be one of Torah and tranquillity; but his outer existence would be one of this-worldly battle with the forces of Reform and assimilation. Moshe Sofer was born on a Friday during the day, and not into the accomplished serenity of *Shabbos*.

The rays of sunlight inched up the walls of the synagogue. Soon *Shabbos* would, of its own accord, begin. There was a clattering, scuffling sound of shoes running down the cobblestone street. Rabbi Abush looked up. Another messenger from Reizl Sofer opened the door to the synagogue.

18

"*Mazel tov*! It's a boy!"

Rabbi Sofer's face broke into a broad smile.

"*Mazel tov*! *Mazel tov*!" the men about him congratulated him warmly and shook his hand.

Rabbi Abush glanced at the cantor and nodded his head. The cantor stood up and turned again to face the rear of the synagogue. "Come in peace, crown of your Husband, Come in joy and in delight; Among the faithful Jewish people, Come, bride, *Shabbos* Queen . . ."

The birth of the baby Moshe, which had held up the coming of the *Shabbos*, now served as the trigger to allow in the peaceful setting of the *Shabbos*, mixed with the joy of his birth.

2

Frankfurt-am-Maim

JEWS HAD LIVED IN FRANKFURT-AM-MAIN, IN WESTERN GERMANY, from as early as the twelfth century, and possibly earlier. In 1462, the Jews were confined to a ghetto, called a *Judengasse*, which was enclosed by walls and gates. As the Jewish population rose into the low thousands, story was added to story, and houses were constructed in back courtyards. Over the years, this *Judengasse* became a long strip of city street within Frankfurt-am-Main where the houses were crazily and haphazardly crowded together, like cliff sides that kept the sun out of the narrow canyon of the street. In a time when buildings were usually no more than two or three stories high, these buildings were piled up story upon story beyond that. In the 1700s, a visitor to the *Judengasse* wrote, "Picture a long street about a mile long, crowded by houses at least five or six stories high. Then picture other houses behind them, all crowded together, with hardly enough yard space to admit any daylight."

Throughout the generations many great rabbis had lived in Frankfurt-am-Main. It is told that until 5450 (1689/90), Rabbi Yeshaiah Horowitz (not the author of *Shnei Luchos Habris*) was chief rabbi. Before he left Frankfurt-am-Main, he posed three difficult Torah questions. He said that whoever answered those questions should be appointed the next chief rabbi.

The community sent three Torah scholars on a mission to find a suitable successor. In the course of their travels, they came to Cracow, Poland, which was a great center of Torah learning. On the day that they arrived, the *bris milah* of a wealthy man's son was being celebrated. The father invited these three scholars to the festive meal. At the meal, the infant's older brother, who was still a boy, delivered a Torah talk. To the scholars' amazement, in the course of his talk, the boy mentioned the same three questions that Rabbi Horowitz had posed; and, even more astonishing, he answered them.

The scholars approached the boy and asked him who his teacher was. The boy pointed to a man, Rabbi Yosef Shmuel, and the scholars went up to him. After introducing themselves, they asked him to accept the role of Chief Rabbi of Frankfurt-am-Main. However, Rabbi Yosef Shmuel refused, saying that he was responsible to his students to remain with them. No matter how strongly the visitors from Frankfurt-am-Main pleaded with him, he would not be persuaded.

Saddened and disappointed, the three scholars left Cracow to seek another candidate for the post.

Shortly afterwards, Rabbi Yosef Shmuel fell gravely ill, so ill that his life hung in the balance, and the *chevrah kaddisha* was summoned. On the eighth day of his illness, when Rabbi Yosef Shmuel saw that he was on the verge of dying, he exclaimed in prayer, "Master of the universe, if You want me to go to Frankfurt-am-Main, then I am ready to do so!"

Almost immediately, he began to slowly recover.

Meanwhile, when the people heard this prayer, they realized that the three visitors from Frankfurt-am-Main had offered this position to Rabbi Yosef Shmuel. Although some time had already passed since they departed, a carriage was sent to follow them.

As it happened, directly after these three scholars had left Cracow, the carriage had broken down and one of them had fallen and injured his hand. As a result, they were now staying in a village that was just two hours outside of Cracow. Since the scholar's hand had by now healed, the three Torah scholars accompanied the people of Cracow back to Rabbi Yosef Shmuel. Soon afterwards, he came with them to Frankfurt-am-Main.

In 1689, Rabbi Yosef Shmuel became Frankfurt-am-Main's chief rabbi.

Rabbi Yosef Shmuel, who could trace his family back to Rabbi Shimon Hadarshan of thirteenth century Frankfurt-am-Main, the author of *Yalkut Shimoni*, learned the entire Talmud forty-two times, in the course of which he corrected various printing errors and made various notes. These notes were eventually printed along with a number of editions of the Talmud.

Rabbi Yosef Shmuel published very little. He felt that many authors were publishing works not for the honor of Torah but for their own sake. In keeping with his request that scholars publish less, Rabbi Yosef Shmuel refrained from publishing his writings.

Rabbi Yosef Shmuel had a son named Moshe. This son married the daughter of the great Torah scholar, Rabbi Shmuel Schotten, the author of *Kos Yeshuos* (a commentary on *Nezikin*), which is studied until this day.

Rabbi Moshe and his wife had a son whom they named

Shmuel. This son was the father of Rabbi Moshe Sofer.

In 5464 (1703/4), Rabbi Yosef Shmuel passed away, and Rabbi Shmuel Schotten succeeded him as Chief Rabbi of Frankfurt-am-Main. He had many students who spread out across Europe and gained high positions as *roshei yeshivos* and *dayanim*.

Following this, a number of other rabbis filled this position: the *Kabbalist*, Rabbi Naftali Hakohein, Rabbi Avraham Brode (author of *Eshel Avraham*), Rabbi Yaakov Kohein (author of *Sheiv Yaakov* and head of a large *yeshivah* where four hundred students learned), Rabbi Yaakov Yehoshua Falk (author of the *P'nei Yehoshua*) and, in 1756, Rabbi Avraham Abush Lissa. He was the chief rabbi of Frankfurt-am-Main at the time that Moshe Sofer was born.

When Shmuel, the son of Rabbi Moshe, grew up, he became an accomplished Torah scholar and made a living as a *sofer*, a scribe of Torah scrolls and *tefillin*. His uncle (his father's brother) Rabbi Yehudah Ashkenazi was the author of the *Be'er Heiteiv* on the *Shulchan Aruch*. Because Rabbi Shmuel worked as a *sofer*, his family name became Sofer, or Sofer (Yiddish-German for "scribe").

Rabbi Shmuel married Reizl, the daughter of a well-known Torah scholar and *Kabbalist* named Rabbi Elchanan, who wrote a *Kabbalistic* commentary on the *siddur*. Reizl was known as a holy and pious woman who collected charity and distributed it among the poor. She was popularly called "Reizl *Tzadeikes*"—Reizl, the pious woman.

In later years, her son Rabbi Moshe Sofer (the Chasam Sofer) spoke of her with the highest praise. Once, after Rabbi Sofer overcame a serious illness, he gave a talk in the middle of which he praised his mother extravagantly, mentioning many of her good qualities. Another time, he told his son Rabbi Shimon that "G-d did nothing of importance without first letting my mother know about it in a dream."

All this merely touches on some of the great Torah leaders who lived in Frankfurt-am-Main in the sixty years until Rabbi Moshe Sofer's birth.

Rabbi Moshe Sofer used to tell a story to illustrate the great level of Torah learning that had been reached in Frankfurt-am-Main.

Years earlier, Rabbi Sofer told, when Frankfurt-am-Main was searching for a chief rabbi, it sent three great Torah scholars to Prague, with which Frankfurt-am-Main had a lively competition as to which was the greater city in Torah learning.

These three rabbis spent the *Shabbos* in Prague, praying at the *Alteneu* Synagogue where, as was the custom, *Shabbos* was brought in early, while the sun was still in the sky. The Friday afternoon prayers were accompanied by singing, led by a conductor who kept the beat by tapping with his foot. This job was given to simple people who were not Torah scholars. Some of the community leaders of Prague decided to play a practical joke, and they offered the most important of the three messengers the dubious honor of leading the singing.

In his ignorance, this rabbi thought that he had been offered a great distinction. Only on *Shabbos* did he learn that he had been the victim of a prank. But he kept his silence.

A year or two later, a traveller came to Prague and entered into discussion with the Chief Rabbi. The Chief Rabbi saw that this man was a Torah scholar, and he invited him to address the congregation on *Shabbos*.

That *Shabbos*, the visitor gave a brilliant, four-hour talk. But then, to the shock of the people, he started singing out the tune that night watchmen call out to remind the people to make sure that nothing catches fire in their houses.

When the people started murmuring, the visitor motioned to them to be quiet, and he addressed them, "Some time ago, when Frankfurt-am-Main was looking for a chief rabbi and sent three representatives here, the community leaders of Prague made one of them into an orchestra conductor.

"Now, I want you to know that I am the night watchman of Frankfurt-am-Main. I just sang to you the tune that I sing out every night. Since you honored me, a simple night watchman, by allowing me to speak in the synagogue, you can imagine how much greater are the representatives that came here."

3

Childhood of Purity

ALONG THE NARROW STREETS OF FRANKFURT-AM-MAIN, A PIOUS woman, her head covered by a tightly drawn kerchief, led a three-year-old child by the hand to *cheder*. Their steps clattered on the ground, and the boy half-ran to keep up with his mother's quick strides. His hand gripped hers tightly so that he would not lose his way. He himself could see nothing of the streets they passed; if there were any unclean animals passing on the street or anything unclean, he could not see them, for his face was veiled.

The people they passed did not wonder at the masked boy's strange appearance. It was the custom of especially pious parents to guard their children's eyes so that between their home and their *yeshivah* nothing would disturb their purity.

"Good morning, Reizl," the woman was greeted by women

in the street leading their own children to school, on the way to the marketplace, or carrying baskets of laundry to the Danube River. Reizl answered their greetings, but she did not slacken her pace. Every day was special, for every day the young child was learning Torah. From beneath his veil, the boy was repeating his lessons to himself. Reizl squeezed his hand. He was a wonder-child. She and Rabbi Shmuel were bringing him up as though he was a gift from G-d, and they were merely G-d's caretakers. Beyond all the goodness and purity with which they had brought him up, he had surpassed them and begun to first respond and then show his own independent spirit of serving G-d.

At the end of *cheder* that day, Moshe's father appeared at the school. "We are going to a great rabbi who is visiting from Metz," his father said. "I will ask him to give you a blessing."

Soon the two were walking along the street, the tall, bearded father, his eyes cast downward, holding the hand of his small child who walked at his side, his face masked, his little shoes scraping along the ground. "His name is Rabbi Aryeh Leib from Metz, Germany," Rabbi Shmuel told his son. "He is a great Torah scholar, and the author of *Sha'agas Aryeh*. It is a great privilege to meet him."

Rabbi Shmuel and his silent son entered the house where Rabbi Aryeh Leib was staying. Moshe heard their steps up the creaking, wooden steps and then he heard a door open. "Oh yes, Rabbi Sofer," he heard a hushed voice of a *shammes*. "Rabbi Aryeh Leib is in the other room. I'll go tell him that you are here."

Rabbi Shmuel drew off Moshe's veil. The waiting room was small and dark, and a splintered table and benches stood alongside one wall. Rabbi Shmuel led Moshe up to the door across the room. The door opened and the short *shammes* came out. "The rabbi will see you now."

Moshe was led by the hand into the next room. The walls

were clean and whitewashed, and through large, airy windows the sunlight streamed in. At a table sat a tall, bearded man, wearing his jacket and a soft, fur hat.

Rabbi Sofer strode forward and as Moshe stood behind silently, introduced himself and the young boy.

"Come here," said Rabbi Aryeh Leib to the quiet child. Moshe stepped forward. "Come," Rabbi Aryeh Leib smiled, "you're quite a shy child."

Rabbi Aryeh Leib put Moshe at ease. He drew Moshe between his knees and spoke to him endearingly. He bent down and stroked Moshe's cheek and played with him. Soon Moshe was laughing and his eyes shone. He liked being with this big man.

"So tell me what you are learning," he asked the little boy. Moshe eagerly lifted his eyes to Rabbi Aryeh Leib and in his childish voice began repeating all his lessons.

Occasionally, the rabbi interrupted the boy to ask a question, and the clever child answered promptly. Moshe enjoyed this man and the questions he was asking.

"Very good, my child," said Rabbi Aryeh Leib. "Very good." He looked up across the sunlit, white room at Rabbi Shmuel standing expectantly. He put his hands on the boy's head and blessed him, and then bent down and kissed him. "Go back to your father, my boy." Moshe went back to his father's side, and he heard Rabbi Aryeh Leib tell his father, "Your son will grow up to become a great tree."

What did that mean, "a great tree"? The words stayed with little Moshe as he and his father took their leave and walked back home. His father repeated the words with pride, and they remained with him for many days, the words of the warm and loving rabbi in the bright, sunny room: that he, little Moshe, would grow up one day to become a "great tree"—he, a little *cheder* boy.

4

In the Path of Torah

WHEN LITTLE MOSHE WAS FOUR YEARS OLD, HE WAS ALREADY learning steadily.

One day, when Moshe came home, he did not say anything, but his father could tell from his face that he was upset.

"What is wrong, Moshe?" his father asked him.

Moshe looked up to seek the warm eyes that he trusted.

"Tell me," his father urged him.

Moshe lowered his eyes and spoke in his vulnerable, child's voice. "We were learning the verse from *Bereishis*, 'And He took dust from the ground.' The *rebbe* translated the verse as 'He took earth from earth.' I asked him, 'Obviously, earth comes from earth. So the verse must be coming to teach us something else in addition.' The *rebbe* grew very angry at me and he didn't say anything. I thought I should ask my question again. When I did, he leaned over and slapped me."

With this memory of his humiliation, Moshe's eyes filled up with tears.

Rabbi Sofer's face grew angry. Moshe didn't know what to expect. "You asked well, Moshe," Rabbi Sofer nodded at him. "Rashi himself was bothered by this question and brought two *midrashim* to answer it. You did well. Go review your learning now."

Although Rabbi Sofer had not expressed his feelings to young Moshe, this episode upset him deeply. Moshe was a wonder-child, a precious jewel, a rare vessel of Torah. He must be watched over, nurtured and cared for like the rarest and most delicate plant. Moshe needed teachers who appreciated him and did not stifle him. One clumsy, heavy-handed teacher could take this special gift and smash it forever. Moshe might still grow up to be a pious, learned adult, but no one would ever know how much had been destroyed.

Rabbi Sofer began to pace across the room. He took control of himself and thought deeply. Before he did anything that affected the boy's future, he must consult with a Torah scholar. "He who takes counsel increases in wisdom" (*Yeshayahu* 28:29). His heart lightened. He would go speak the matter over with Rabbi Nassan Adler.

Rabbi Nassan Adler was one of Frankfurt-am-Main's greatest Torah scholars. Among other teachers, he had learned under Rabbi Yehoshua Falk, author of the *Pnei Yehoshua*. He was also a great *Kabbalist*, and although he had many customs contrary to those of the community, no one questioned his authority.

Rabbi Sofer went to Rabbi Adler and tersely described how Moshe's teacher had acted, without betraying his passionate feelings.

Rabbi Adler took a deep breath. His equanimity calmed the angry spirit of Rabbi Sofer. "If you have been blessed with such a gifted son," he said, "why don't you yourself fulfill the *mitzvah* of teaching Torah? As the verse says, 'And you shall teach your children.' Take the boy to your side and learn with him together."

Rabbi Sofer listened to Rabbi Adler in silence. "Yes," he murmured, "I shall heed your words."

Rabbi Sofer took Moshe out of the *cheder* and, setting aside as many of his own concerns as possible, applied himself to teaching Moshe Torah.

Rabbi Sofer learned with his son in this way for two years. When Moshe learned the laws of blessings, he learned that there was a question of what blessing to make over sugar. Although he loved sweet things, when he became aware that there was a question involved, he decided that for the sake of the Torah he must hold himself back. From that point on and for the rest of his life, he never allowed himself sweets.

Moshe learned with his father every day. At night, when Moshe lay down to go to sleep, Rabbi Sofer asked him a question about what they had learned that day. Before Moshe was allowed to fall asleep, he had to answer his father. If he drifted off, his father would awaken him until he succeeded in answering. For the sake of the Torah, little Moshe had to hold himself back from sleep.

When Moshe was six years old, his father brought him to the *beis midrash* of a very pious Torah scholar named Rabbi Zalman Chassid (Zalman the pious one). A very wealthy man, Rabbi Zalman Chassid had decided to set aside his business and devote his life to learning and teaching Torah. He had a garden in which he would learn in the summer, basking in the warm sunshine and delighting in the bird songs that mingled with the voices of his students learning Torah. In the garden stood a cottage that contained a heated *mikveh*.

By the time Moshe turned seven, he had already been learning *Gemara* for an appreciable while, and he knew several tractates by heart. When he completed the tractate of

Beitzah, he gave a talk at the festive meal in which he linked the end of the tractate to its beginning. This was such a mature analysis of the *Gemara* that many years later, he repeated it to his students, who then studied it in depth and were amazed when he told them that he had created it when he had been a little boy.

This speech made Moshe famous throughout Frankfurt-am-Main. Word of his prowess passed through the city, sparking conversation or acknowledgement in admiring silence.

A year later, when Moshe was eight years old, his father brought him to Rabbi Moshe Margolies to test Moshe's learning abilities. Rabbi Margolies, the author of the *Pnei Moshe*, lived in the Land of Israel, but was visiting Frankfurt-am-Main.

In the high-ceilinged *beis midrash*, Rabbi Margolies directed Moshe to learn a page of *Gemara* together with its commentaries, and to come back later to be tested. Moshe and his father left the room of the great rabbi, and Rabbi Sofer left his son alone to learn the text. After Moshe learned the *Gemara*, he appeared again before Rabbi Margolies. Rabbi Margolies asked him various questions, and young Moshe answered every question with deliberation and clarity.

"I am afraid you may have received help from your father in preparing this page," Rabbi Moshe Margolies commented.

Moshe said nothing.

Rabbi Margolies opened a page of *Gemara* dealing with sacrifices, which is usually not learned and is considered difficult and esoteric. This time, he insisted that the boy learn the page in his presence, so that he could not be helped by anyone.

Fortunately, most of Moshe's learning with his father had been in this area, and the material was familiar to him. When Rabbi Margolies tested Moshe, he spoke as firmly and clearly as he had done earlier.

Rabbi Margolies was deeply impressed both with young Moshe's abilities in learning and his evident piety. "Call your father, dear boy," he told Moshe. "I wish to speak to him."

Moshe called his father into the *beis midrash*. Moshe stood at the back of the *beis midrash* and watched his father and Rabbi Margolies sit down. He saw their lips moving, but he could not hear what they were saying.

"Your son is a very gifted child," said Rabbi Margolies to Rabbi Sofer. "I propose that you let me be his teacher. He will return with me to Eretz Yisrael and I will take care of him as though I am his father."

Rabbi Sofer said little, but in his heart he rejoiced. That his Moshe should become the personal ward and student of such a great Torah scholar! It was a rare honor. He nodded his head and smiled slightly. "You honor me," he said. "I am prepared to heed your words, but I must also hear what my wife has to say."

Rabbi Margolies said nothing but went back to his studies.

At home, young Moshe watched his parents discuss his future. Rabbi Sofer thought it a wonderful idea that Moshe should go with Rabbi Margolies. "He is a great rabbi, but that is not all. Our son will have the privilege of growing up in the Holy Land. The *Gemara* says, 'Whoever lives in the Land of Israel is without sin.'"

But Moshe saw that his mother was not persuaded by his father's words. She shook her head. "Moshe is only eight years old and still a child. Let him remain here and be a child to me. Let him stay so that I can be a mother to him."

Rabbi Sofer argued but Moshe's mother was adamant. "Eretz Yisrael is a great privilege, but our Moshe will grow to his full greatness here outside the land. Eretz Yisrael will have to be withheld from him."

Moshe understood that his parents were arguing over his fate. But he held himself back. He would allow them to determine what direction his life should take.

His mother won the argument, and Moshe remained in Frankfurt-am-Main. Perhaps it was this episode that planted in him the first shoots of his deep and abiding love for Eretz Yisrael. "Even though we are in exile against our will," he once wrote, "only our bodies are here, but not our thoughts. Wherever we are, in our thoughts we are upon our holy soil."

The next year, when Moshe was only nine years old, his father sent him to learn in the *beis midrash* of Rabbi Nassan Adler.

Rabbi Adler was a Torah scholar with unusually wide-ranging interests. He was a great expert in the *Kabbalah*, as well as the Talmud and other parts of Torah. He was also very knowledgeable about Hebrew and Aramaic grammar, and the natural sciences. He was known as a very pious, good and humble person. Rabbi Adler told his students not to call him "Rabbi," but simply "Mr." He spoke quietly and pleasantly to everyone. He declared all of his possessions ownerless, so that if someone were to take something of his, he would not be guilty of theft.

Day and night, with the exception of the eve of *Shabbos* and holidays, his house was open to all visitors. One could drop in at any hour and find visitors of all kinds, students and rabbis, *Kabbalists* and *Talmudic* scholars, visiting, discussing anything under the sun or esoteric matters that were beyond the sphere of the celestial bodies.

He was very strict with himself. He was always awake at midnight, and he had very strict standards of *kashrus* and the laws of ritual impurity.

Some said that the spirit of G-d spoke through Rabbi Adler. In later years, Rabbi Chaim Halberstam (author of *Divrei Chaim*) said of him that "I heard from my holy teacher, Rabbi Naftali of Ropschitz, who heard from the author of *Noam Elimelech* that other than the soul of the Baal Shem Tov, for many years such a holy soul had not descended into this world."

But although Rabbi Adler was widely renowned, some people found it hard to appreciate him. This was apparently due to his unusual ways in serving G-d.

Although Rabbi Adler was warm to his coterie of students, his teachings were not well-known outside their circles because he refused to write down any of his teachings. He believed that one may only write down one's Torah thoughts if one is afraid that he will forget them. However, Rabbi Adler had such a strong memory that he felt that he had no right to write down any of his Torah insights.

Besides this, the yearning of Rabbi Adler's soul for total G-dliness caused him to follow many unusual customs. These customs formed a barrier between him and the community of Frankfurt-am-Main, and made it difficult for people to appreciate his warmth and breadth.

Rabbi Adler prayed according to the *nussach* of the Ari, even as cantor. Every morning, Rabbi Adler (who was a *kohein*), as well as the other *kohanim* in his *minyan*, blessed the people every morning, as is done in *Eretz Yisrael*. He said that when the Beis Hamikdash would be rebuilt, he would very much want to perform the service of the *kohein gadol*. He was fluent in the laws relating to the Beis Hamikdash. Rabbi Adler pronounced Hebrew according to the Sephardic pronunciation. He learned this from a Jerusalem rabbi, Rabbi Chaim Modai, who had lived in his house for two or three years.

Every *Shabbos*, Rabbi Adler went up to the Torah twice; both as *kohein* and for *maftir*.

Subsequently, Rabbi Adler's unique customs were the cause of strife between him and the other members of the community. But for the time being, their relations were cordial.

35

In later years, Rabbi Moshe Sofer remembered Rabbi Adler with great respect and affection. Once, at a meeting of Torah scholars, one rabbi commented that Rabbi Adler had been an angel of G-d. "What do you mean, only an angel?" Rabbi Moshe Sofer immediately retorted.

Another time, Rabbi Moshe Sofer commented to his son Shimon, "Without exaggeration, no angel was as proficient in the pathways of heaven as Rabbi Adler was." (Rabbi Shimon Sofer had asked his father about Rabbi Adler for a biography that he was writing. Unfortunately, this biography has been lost.)

Moshe studied very hard in Rabbi Adler's *yeshivah*. From the age of ten, he got up every night after midnight to learn Torah. Going through the *Gemara* consistently in this way, he completed the entire Talmud in depth at the age of sixteen. Moshe was not only a diligent student, but a creative thinker as well. In later years, he said that from the time he had gained the ability to think independently about Torah, not a day went by that he did not create Torah insights.

Moshe grew very close to Rabbi Adler. He studied every movement and every statement that Rabbi Adler made. Even though he was still quite young, he learned on the same level of deep understanding as the older students.

Rabbi Adler's greatness was a necessary catalyst to develop the still immature virtuosity of young Moshe. Rabbi Chaim Halberstam commented in later years, "It is not so remarkable that Rabbi Moshe Sofer should have become such a great and holy person, since his teacher was Rabbi Nassan Adler." And Rabbi Moshe himself often commented, "I was a true student to my teacher. I chopped wood for him and drew water for him, and this has stood me in good stead." And he would tell his students, "I was a different type of student than you, for I had a different type of *rebbe*."

5

Apprenticeship

RABBI NASSAN ADLER, DRESSED IN HIS *SHABBOS* CLOTHING, SAT IN his private study. His new student, the ten-year-old wonder-child Moshe, would soon be giving his talk. Rabbi Adler was proud of the boy.

In the *beis midrash*, Moshe sat at the plain, wooden table as other students and Torah scholars filed into the room. Moshe heard a familiar voice. He lifted his eyes and met the eyes of his father. His father nodded slightly and Moshe looked down again.

In addition to the *yeshivah's* regular learning schedule, at the end of the week, every student learned a topic on his own. On *Shabbos*, one of the students would give a talk on that topic and present his original insights. Today it was Moshe's turn.

Someone sat down at the empty space a few seats from

Moshe. Moshe looked up. It was his father. Moshe stood up and began to present his talk. It was a talk on a topic in the *Gemara*, filled with complex arguments. Moshe was confident in his abilities and his arguments. He spoke smoothly and with confidence. He glanced up and saw that everyone was listening attentively and following his words. At his side, his father seemed to be wearing an expression of muted pleasure and approval.

Moshe had now come to a point in his talk in which he dealt with a difficult question that had been posed by his mother's father Rabbi Shmuel Schotten. Moshe took a breath, glanced about him and, after a pause, continued smoothly, "but with all due respect, my grandfather made a mistake on this point, because this really isn't a difficult question at all."

Rabbi Shmuel Sofer jerked forward in surprise and anger. What? What did he say? This boy must be taught respect! He may be a wonder-child, but he must learn how to restrain himself! How dare he speak that way about his holy and scholarly grandfather? Rabbi Sofer reached his hand out and for a split second looked into the startled eyes of his young son. Then he slapped him soundly across the face.

Moshe opened his mouth. He remained silent. His face turned pale white, and then his entire face turned crimson.

Moshe's father said nothing, and the others at the table sat in shocked silence. There was only the sound of Moshe scraping his seat back and, with his head lowered, walking out of the *beis midrash*, leaving an empty seat at the table.

An hour later, Rabbi Adler heard the footsteps of his students in the hall—then a knock on the door, skittering, it seemed, diffident.

The students outside the door stood nervous and anxious. From within, they heard Rabbi Adler call, "Come in!"

The white door swung open. Rabbi Adler's eyes met those of the student who had knocked. He closed the large volume of the *Gemara* he had been learning and his hand ran along its rough cloth exterior.

There was a silence.

"How did Moshe do in his speech today?" asked Rabbi Adler.

The student who had knocked stepped forward before Rabbi Adler and remained standing. The other two students stood by the door. They watched the student tell Rabbi Adler how Moshe had spoken and then been silenced. They saw Rabbi Adler's eyes shine intensely—in anger, perhaps, or in concern for the boy. They could not tell.

Rabbi Adler waved his hand in a dismissing gesture. His eyes gazed down at the rough, green cloth of the *Gemara*. "Thank you."

The student stepped back and the two other students, seeing that the interview was over, turned and opened the white door.

As they were leaving, they heard from behind them, "Send Moshe in."

They turned to see Rabbi Adler's fathomless eyes. Then they turned back, rubbing against the smooth, painted door. A few moments later, Moshe entered Rabbi Adler's room and stood before Rabbi Adler.

"Sit down, Moshe." Moshe sat down and said nothing.

"I was told about your talk today. Your father is concerned that you do not become too self-assured in your learning. He does not want you to become like many other clever *yeshivah* students who think they are much greater than they are. Egotism is a very great character flaw.

"But your father does not know you as I do. He does not know your true humility or your true expertise in Torah.

"The honor that a student owes his teacher is greater than the honor that a son owes his father. As your teacher, and for the sake of your becoming all that you can be, I cannot let your

39

father, even though he loves you and even though he is a Torah scholar, continue to treat you this way.

"He is like a farmer who knows how to raise barley but not wheat. What is good for the barley will destroy the wheat. Your father would be a fine model for an ordinary, very talented son. But I tell you that you have more than talent. Your gifts must not be ruined by anyone, no matter who he is and no matter how well-meaning he is.

"Therefore, Moshe, love and respect him for he is your father but do not discuss with him."

"Yes, Rabbi."

"You may go."

Moshe walked home with heavy steps. He was a little boy of ten, and must he never discuss Torah with his father again, for years and years? But Rabbi Adler had spoken and he was right. This step must be taken.

When Moshe got home, he reported to his mother, as his father listened on, to what Rabbi Nassan had said.

"I will not protest," Rabbi Shmuel responded. "Rabbi Adler is now the boy's teacher, and we will do what he commands. Seven years ago, I took Moshe away from his teacher for being too strict, and now Rabbi Adler will do the same to me. It is for the sake of the boy's learning and I will not protest."

Soon after this, Moshe left his parents' home and went to live with Rabbi Adler. Now the bond between Moshe and his teacher grew stronger than ever.

Although Moshe was to have other teachers as well, Rabbi Adler remained his principal teacher. Moshe lived with Rabbi Adler, ate with him, travelled with him and carefully studied all of his actions and customs. In later years, Rabbi Moshe wrote, "My hand did not move from his, and I learned all of his ways."

Rabbi Adler was more than just a teacher to Moshe. He

seems to have been very much a father to the boy, especially after Moshe lived in his house.

But Moshe did not receive only uncritical love from Rabbi Adler. Once, when Moshe offered a highly original interpretation that was not well-founded, the only response he received from Rabbi Adler was silence. Moshe returned to his studies until he himself was able to discover the error that he had made.

At the same time, Moshe also began learning with Rabbi Pinchas Horowitz, author of *Sefer Haflaah*, a classic of *halachic pilpul*. Rabbi Horowitz (1730-1805) had come from Cracow to become Chief Rabbi of Frankfurt-am-Main in 1771, two years after the death of the previous Chief Rabbi, Avraham Abush. According to *chassidic* tradition, Rabbi Horowitz had been a student of Rabbi Dov Ber of Mezhirich, who had been leader of the *chassidic* movement. He was also said to have been on good terms with Rabbi Shneur Zalman, the founder of *Chabad Chassidism*. His brother, Rabbi Shmuel "Shmelke" Horowitz, later became rabbi of Nikolsburg. Rabbi Pinchas Horowitz had his own private *minyan* where, Rabbi Moshe Sofer reported in later years, he prayed according to the *nussach* of the Ari, like Rabbi Adler.

Rabbi Horowitz was on good terms with Rabbi Adler. Whenever he had a difficult question in Torah, he would go to Rabbi Adler to consult with him. Once, Rabbi Adler told him, "It isn't right that you, the rabbi of the city, should come to the house of a simple layman like myself. You do not need my Torah or my advice. But if you nevertheless want to speak with me, call me and I will come to you, even in the middle of the night."

Moshe valued Rabbi Horowitz very greatly, and learned very diligently with him. In return, Rabbi Horowitz had very warm feelings for Moshe, and treated him as an especially beloved student.

In later years, Rabbi Moshe often cited the actions of both rabbis as a basis for his *halachic* decisions. Once, for instance, his father-in-law Rabbi Akiva Eiger asked him if one is allowed to comb one's sidelocks. Rabbi Moshe Sofer replied that he had seen Rabbi Adler do so, and it must in consequence be permitted. Then, on the basis of Rabbi Adler's action, he searched for the source of the *halachah* in the Talmud.

Moshe also recorded very carefully everything that Rabbi Horowitz did and said, even in the course of a casual conversation. In later years he wrote, "I once heard something from Rabbi Horowitz that he mentioned on *Purim*. Even though he mentioned it as a *Purim* witticism, it appears to me that since these words were uttered by a holy man, they are not devoid of content, G-d forbid."

Both Rabbi Adler and Rabbi Horowitz were involved in the study of *Kabbalah*. But neither of them ever mentioned the *Zohar* in a discourse. The community in Germany was suspicious of mysticism, and it was unwise to discuss it in public.

In later years, Rabbi Moshe Sofer would often mention these two Torah giants together. He once wrote, "I am astonished that a person who knows the worth of Rabbi Adler and Rabbi Horowitz, men who combined greatness and modesty, and who now sees to what a low state the world has fallen, can continue living."

Once, when Moshe was thirteen years old, Rabbi Yehudah of Lissa, author of *Mareh Kohein*, visited Frankfurt-am-Main with the intention of publishing his work there. He asked Rabbi Adler to send him a well-learned and capable student to proofread the manuscript before it went to the printer.

Rabbi Adler sent Moshe to review the manuscript. When he came in, Rabbi Yehudah of Lissa asked him, "What do you want, little boy?"

"Rabbi Adler sent me to help you look over the manuscript," Moshe replied.

"What? Please go home. I think there is some mistake." Rabbi Yehudah was very upset. Was Rabbi Adler playing a practical joke on him? To send him a *bar-mitzvah* boy? He himself went immediately to Rabbi Adler and rebuked him to his face. "Why do you make fun of me? What have I done that you have decided to treat me with such disrespect?"

"You are quite mistaken," Rabbi Adler replied. "I in no way meant to insult you. This young boy is more than competent to help you review your manuscript."

Rabbi Yehudah of Lissa was appeased and consented to let Moshe go through his work.

At about that time, Moshe concentrated on learning the difficult *halachos* of purity and impurity (*tumah vetaharah*). He ultimately gained a reputation of being one of the greatest experts of his time in this field. Besides this, Moshe learned a great deal from Rabbi Yehudah of Lissa and in later years, listed him as one of his teachers. (Other teachers whom he mentioned were Rabbi Mendel Lillig and Rabbi Nassan, author of *Binyan Shlomo*.)

6

To Learn in Mainz

THE EARLY MORNING WIND BLEW THE DANK, COLD MIST AGAINST Moshe's face and swirled behind him. When he looked back from the carriage in which he rode, he saw the great city of Frankfurt-am-Main already being swallowed into the fog. Fog behind him, and the road ahead of him stretching blindly into the white, faceless fog! Only his meager suitcase of belongings in the wagon, the back of the wagon driver and the bay horse with his downcast head plodding slowly forward on the clay ground seemed to have any reality.

Behind him, obscured by the mist, lay his home, his parents, his *beis midrash* and teachers. Before him lay the *yeshivah* of Mainz, headed by the great rabbis, Rabbi Michel Sheyer and Rabbi Tevele. Would he do well there? What kind of men were they? All was uncertain, all unclear.

The horse strayed to the side of the road to crop at a sprig of grass, but the wagon driver yanked at the rein and growled, and the horse reluctantly turned its head back to the road, and plodded forward. So too must he, Moshe, force himself forward, force himself to keep going, remind himself why he had not stayed with his teachers, his friends, his family.

For three years, from the age of ten to thirteen, Moshe had lived with Rabbi Adler, learning Torah from him and other great rabbis.

But wherever he turned, Moshe ran into his father; perhaps it was in the synagogue or in the *beis midrash*, or simply on the street. Moshe loved his father and wanted to grow close to him. Certainly, his father would not again rebuke him. But there was always his teacher's admonition!

And how could he go visit his family, how could he visit his beloved mother, and not discuss all he had learned with his father? Should he sneak in when his father was not there? Or should he come at any time and simply not exchange a word with him? Always he thought of his father. And whenever their eyes met, whenever Moshe would see his back on the street, whenever Moshe would want to run up to him, to share a word with him, to sit at the table and speak with him, he was brought up short by his teacher's admonition!

Finally, Moshe could bear the constant emotional turmoil no longer. He decided to leave Frankfurt-am-Main and begin a life where the pain of his severance from his father was not constantly before him.

And so the long journey, driving through a tunnel of deep fog, had begun.

When Moshe came to Mainz after a few days' journey, night was falling. The sky was clear, and the gentle stars shone like pearls upon crushed indigo. A warm breeze blew against his face, and blew past him snatches of noises and talk from the town that lay before him.

In Mainz itself, Moshe was cordially received. He was

45

given a room in the house of a wealthy man. This man showed Moshe his large library of *sefarim* and invited Moshe to use them whenever he wished.

The next day, Moshe presented himself to Rabbi Sheyer, bringing with him letters of introduction from his rabbis in Frankfurt-am-Main.

Everyone in Mainz was quite welcoming. Moshe's sterling reputation had preceded him, and he was given all the facilities he needed to learn with as few distractions as possible.

At that time, French soldiers were billeted with various city residents. Among them was a young French officer named Pauli de Monfort, who was staying in the same house as Moshe. This officer offered to do Moshe's household chores in return for Moshe's teaching him German. This arrangement led to a friendly relationship, and the officer grew to have a very positive appreciation of Torah.

It is possibly at this period that Moshe learned at least the basics of his far-ranging knowledge in various topics such as mathematics, astronomy, physics and anatomy. Possibly, he learned his knowledge of French from this soldier. Studying from works written by Torah scholars, Moshe applied himself to learning all the sciences and fields of knowledge that would broaden his ability to understand Torah. In addition to the sciences, Moshe also gained an understanding of history, politics and cartography. He also became well-versed in languages, and in addition to German, he learned French and Latin.

A year after Moshe's arrival, Rabbi Sheyer honored the boy with a document certifying him to be *"meshuchrar"*—freed. This was a sign of great respect. For the *halachah* states that a student is obligated to serve his teacher in various ways. However, a teacher may, if he so chooses, free his student of those obligations. This was the meaning of the document that

Moshe had now received. It indicated Rabbi Sheyer's feeling that Moshe could no longer be considered a simple student.

This document had a practical application as well. Now Moshe was entitled to receive a regular income from the community fund and from individual householders.

But Moshe was not satisfied. He had all that he had sought, but the ache within him had not subsided. The ache in his heart would not go away, and his feelings and his need for warmth, for family, for home could not be denied. He was welcome here in Mainz, he was well-treated. He had everything—except for home. He wished to go back to his teacher Rabbi Adler. And he yearned to see his family again.

Moshe was sitting in the *beis midrash* late at night by the light of a candle whose drooping, charred head was the source of an uneven flame. He looked up from his *sefer* at the candle. What were they doing now in Frankfurt-am-Main? Were all the students awake in Rabbi Adler's *beis midrash*, learning together? Moshe stood up and walked to the door of the *beis midrash*. He stepped into the silent street. He gazed at the impersonal and glittering sky. A falling star, like a glowing, milky pearl, swooped down in silence, blazed for an instant, and then, silently, faded invisibly into blackness.

Would he fade into nothingness here in Mainz? Or would his aching heart fade finally and leave nothing but a hollowness inside him if he ignored his pain?

Moshe stepped back indoors and hurried to the flame. He must trim it now if it was to continue burning.

The next day, Moshe announced to Rabbi Sheyer that he was returning to Frankfurt-am-Main. He had learned in Mainz for two years. He had taken his first steps to independence. Now it was time to go home.

7

Return to Frankfurt

THE LONG ROWS OF PEPPER AND CUCUMBER STRETCHED OUT ON either side of the road, red and green vegetables hanging among the leaves in the fields beneath the bright afternoon sky.

Little clouds of dust flew up in the footsteps of the *yeshivah* students strolling outside the gates of Frankfurt-am-Main.

Moshe had been back home for a year. Continuing his rigorous learning schedule, he had completed the entire Talmud.

"What should I do to celebrate the *siyum*?" he had asked Rabbi Adler at the beginning of the week.

"You should fast for three days in a row," Rabbi Adler had instructed Moshe, "eating in the evenings."

Today was the third fast day, and Moshe and a few of his

fellow-students had spent the day walking through the refreshing rural roads that lay outside the crowded neighborhood of Jewish Frankfurt-am-Main.

The sun hung low above the horizon like a globular yellow pepper hanging upon its branch. The western sky was ribbed with ruddy clouds like rough, rich soil.

"We'll have to say *Minchah* here," said one of the students. "We'll never get back to the *beis midrash* in time."

While the students stood silent in the middle of *Shmoneh Esrei*, a large, rough farmer came down the road, his hoe slung over his massive shoulder.

"Jews, eh?" he shouted, swinging the hoe down from his shoulder. "Get off the road and go back to your *Judengasse*!" He advanced on them, raising the hoe like a bludgeon. All the students ran away, except for Moshe, who stood still, continuing his prayer.

The other students looked back and watched from a distance.

"I told you, move!" the farmer shouted, and he strode up to Moshe and raised his hand to beat him.

Moshe swiftly struck the farmer once, and the man fell to the ground, unconscious. Moshe's strength was not merely physical. By his own admission in later years, he was at that time more familiar with the literature of *Kabbalah* than many acknowledged *Kabbalists*.

The stars were already surfacing when the students returned to Frankfurt-am-Main, and Moshe was the hero of his fellow-students.

It is hard to know whether in the year since Moshe had returned to Frankfurt-am-Main, his prayers had been answered. He had returned to learn with his teachers and to see his family and friends, but he could still not speak to his father.

One day, as Moshe sat in the *beis midrash*, a woman sitting upstairs in the women's section reciting *Tehillim* saw through the lattice a man come in and walk up to Moshe. The man merely murmured and she could not hear what he was saying. Moshe grasped the man's arm and burst into a sob: "Father, my father!"

At the age of sixteen, Moshe was orphaned. He had never had the chance to be close to his father since the age of ten. Moshe mourned his father deeply. It is striking that even in later life, Rabbi Moshe Sofer never mentioned his father in any of his response. He kept his silence for the extent of his life.

8

Conflicts

THE BLAST OF THE *SHOFAR* SOUNDED THROUGH THE *BEIS MIDRASH* and into the quiet night. Under Rabbi Adler's direction, Moshe put the *shofar* to his lips and blew again.

Rabbi Adler and his students had been learning in the *beis midrash* that evening as usual when downstairs, on the first floor, a rowdy newly-wed couple entered their apartment. The man was boisterous and probably drunk, and his bride too was loud and raucous. Their shrieks and laughter burst through the *beis midrash*.

"Moshe," Rabbi Adler told the sixteen-year-old student, "go downstairs and tell the couple that they are disturbing our learning. Tell them to put an end to their rowdiness and to be on their way."

The man who opened the door to Moshe's knock was flushed and there was a smell of whiskey on his breath.

"Quiet? Your rabbi wants us to be quiet? We'll be as loud as we want for as long as we want, you tell him that!"

Moshe went back upstairs and the noise from below continued.

"Go down again and tell them to be quiet or they will regret it," Rabbi Adler instructed Moshe.

Again Moshe went downstairs and knocked on the door. "Oh, it's you again!" the drunk bridegroom slurred his words. Behind him, Moshe could see the woman's coarse laughing face. She called out, "Tell him to go—"

"I'll tell him where to go!" the man interrupted her. "You listen to me—"

"My rabbi said that if you do not leave now, you will regret it."

"And you tell your rabbi that if he sends you down here to bother me again, I'll beat the living daylights out of you!" Moshe heard the woman burst into a gale of laughter, and the man slammed the door in his face.

Moshe went upstairs and reported the bridegroom's threat to Rabbi Adler. But soon, when the noise started anew, Rabbi Adler again nodded to Moshe.

"Please . . .," he said.

For the third time, Moshe descended to the downstairs apartment.

He knocked at the door and the man swung it open. "What do you want?"

"My rabbi told me to tell you—"

The man's hand swung up swiftly and smashed Moshe across the face. A sudden clap of pain seared Moshe's cheek, and he staggered back. Then the door slammed in his face.

Moshe shook his head and heavily came back upstairs.

"What happened?" asked Rabbi Adler when Moshe appeared at the door, staggering slightly.

"I did as you asked me," Moshe replied, speaking thickly.

When he stepped forward, Rabbi Adler saw the mark of the blow on his face.

It was at this point that Rabbi Adler realized what had happened, and what coarse and corrupt people were downstairs. It was then that Rabbi Adler had ordered Moshe to blow the *shofar*.

People nearby wondered, what was going on. Everyone knew that a *shofar* was blown during the year only on the rarest occasions. What mystical practices was Rabbi Adler, the strange, *Kabbalistic* rabbi, engaging in?

The next day, before twenty-four hours had passed, the young couple fell ill and died.

The news spread like wildfire through the city. Rabbi Adler had used his *Kabbalistic* powers to kill young newlyweds! And not any newly-wed couple either. It turned out that both the bridegroom and the bride were members of two of Frankfurt-am-Main's most wealthy and powerful Jewish families.

Indignation spread throughout the city. Rabbi Adler must be punished. He must be taught a lesson. All the suspicions and misgivings that people had about Rabbi Adler throughout the years because of his unusual customs and *Kabbalistic* leanings now came to a boil with this scandalous episode.

Rabbi Adler was a mystic and a wonder-worker in a city that did not relish tales of miracles. Without his approval, his admirers had spread the tales of wonders that they had witnessed. The city did not approve. Torah is based on learning Talmud and on piety, not on strange and supernatural going-on! And more than that, some of Rabbi Adler's students had grown heady with the mystical atmosphere that suffused the *beis midrash*. They began to tell their dreams in public, announcing them as prophetic and apocalyptic visions.

Some of the people of Frankfurt-am-Main were afraid that Rabbi Adler might be a follower of Shabbesai Tzvi, the false

messiah. Although more than a hundred years had passed
since Shabbesai Tzvi had converted to Islam, there were still
secret groups of believers in Poland and Germany. Didn't
Rabbi Adler have strange customs? And weren't some of those
customs identical to what that new and controversial group,
the *chassidim*, was doing? And didn't some people suspect
that the *chassidim* too might be a Shabbesai Tzvi-like sect?

That Rabbi Adler was known to be a pious and holy Jew
mattered nothing now. If they had considered the matter, the
people might have concluded that when such a holy man
engaged in a mystical ceremony that resulted in someone's
punishment, the punishment was just. But people were
outraged. Those who had always been suspicious of him now
joined together with the couple's families, who were influen-
tial in Frankfurt. Action had to be taken! There was even talk
of handing Rabbi Adler over to the non-Jewish authorities to
try him.

Rabbi Horowitz saw that the affair was erupting into a
public scandal that must be stopped. Although he was a close
friend of Rabbi Adler, he dispatched a delegation of twenty-
four Torah scholars to require that Rabbi Adler accept upon
himself a ban of excommunication.

But Rabbi Adler refused and sent them away from his door.

An announcement was made in all the synagogues that it
was forbidden to pray in Rabbi Adler's *minyan*, and that
whoever violated the decree would be excommunicated.

Rabbi Adler paid this decree no heed and continued to
lead his private *minyan*.

Soon afterwards, another decree was passed declaring
that Rabbi Adler had no right to maintain a *minyan* but must
go pray in one of the city synagogues under the supervision of
the city leaders; and that if he did not obey this decree, he
would himself be excommunicated. In order to help maintain
Rabbi Adler's honor, all private *minyan*im were banned,

besides the one in the *yeshivah*. In addition, Rabbi Adler was not allowed to engage in any rabbinical functions or to make any legal decisions. This decree was signed by Rabbi Horowitz and other leaders.

Again, Rabbi Horowitz appealed to Rabbi Adler, urging him to accept the ban for the sake of putting an end to the controversy.

In response to this second appeal, Rabbi Adler accepted a ban of excommunication for a period of six weeks. This succeeded in calming down the situation.

After the six-week period was over, when the Torah scholars came to Rabbi Adler to absolve him of his excommunication, he read them the six weekly Torah portions of the previous six weeks.

Throughout all this controversy, Moshe Sofer continued to stand firmly by Rabbi Adler's side. Nothing could sway him to believe anything disparaging about his great rabbi, whose piety and holiness Moshe saw at every moment. Even though Rabbi Adler had unusual customs that met with opposition, Moshe saw that they were a legitimate expression of Rabbi Adler's heartfelt service of G-d. Nothing could weaken Moshe's faith in his teacher.

Calm returned to Frankfurt-am-Main and again Rabbi Adler was free to lead his *yeshivah*. But the atmosphere still was strained, and Rabbi Adler felt stifled. In this way, three years passed.

In 5542 (1781/2), Rabbi Adler sat at his study and slit open an envelope that had arrived from Boskowitz, an old and prestigious Jewish community in Moravia. He unfolded the stiff paper and bent over the spiked, elegant lettering. It was an invitation from the fathers of the city to become their rabbi. Rabbi Adler leaned back in his chair and nodded slightly, his fathomless eyes gazing out in thought.

9

Journey to Boskowitz

A GROUP OF TORAH SCHOLARS AND STUDENTS HUDDLED ABOUT THE fine carriage in the brisk early morning.

"Bless me, rabbi."

A hand reached out from the open door of the carriage. One of the men grasped the hand and kissed it.

"Rabbi Adler, bless me, please."

Rabbi Adler placed his hand on a student's head. He leaned over and murmured into the student's ear. When he removed his hand, the student backed reverentially away.

Rabbi Adler's eyes roamed across the faces of the men standing on the road at the outskirts of Frankfurt-am-Main. He caught Moshe Sofer's eye.

"Moshe!" he said. "What blessing do you want?"

"I want to see my teacher's face in Boskowitz," Moshe replied without hesitation.

His *rebbe*, mentor and instructor since childhood was leaving to become rabbi of Boskowitz. Moshe wanted to accompany him, but Rabbi Adler had told him that he must remain behind. Boskowitz was far from Frankfurt-am-Main, with only a small number of scholars, and Moshe must stay in a center of Torah learning. Moshe had tried to reconcile himself to their parting, but he still yearned to remain with Rabbi Adler.

Rabbi Adler gave Moshe his blessing. Soon, he closed the carriage door, and his face was hidden behind the small, dark window. The carriage driver snapped his whip, and the two horses reared their heads and trotted forward.

Behind the carriage walked a small group of people carrying a Torah scroll. In his piety, Rabbi Adler did not want to carry the scroll with him in the carriage. The scroll was therefore relayed by foot from town to town.

Slowly, Moshe turned his footsteps home, the wind whipping in his face. But as he trudged back to the familiar streets and houses and saw again in his mind's eye his parting from Rabbi Adler, he realized that when he had asked to see Rabbi Adler in Boskowitz, he had not added, *b'li neder*—"without a vow." Rabbi Yeshaiah Horowitz, Moshe recalled, had written in *Shnei Luchos Habris* that one should add these words whenever one mentioned something that one meant to do. It might well be that Moshe had made a vow to go to Boskowitz.

A stone was lifted from Moshe's heart. He would again be able to see Rabbi Adler, whose face and presence were the center of his life! Before, he had to obey Rabbi Adler's refusal, but now, he must go—according to *halachah* there was an obligation.

This time he would not hold himself back. He must let nothing get in his way. He had made a vow and he must fulfill it immediately. He had lost the presence of his true teacher, and he must regain it at once.

Moshe turned around and began striding after Rabbi Adler.

He turned his back on Frankfurt-am-Main and he turned his face to his teacher of Torah. He was leaving without taking along a single shred of clothing, without a single *sefer*. But no matter, for he was going to his teacher of Torah. He was leaving without visiting his father's grave. But no matter, for he was going to his teacher of life. He was leaving without parting from his friends or from Rabbi Horowitz. He was striding firmly out of Frankfurt-am-Main without even saying good-bye to his beloved, pious mother. His soul told him that this time he must not hold himself back. He must again be embraced and revived by the holy presence of his teacher.

As Moshe strode down the road, a friend met him and began walking with him. Outside the city, several young gentile toughs accosted them. One of them stepped up to Moshe's side and attempted to strike him. Moshe struck him so hard that he ran off. But now the other toughs chased after him. Carrying his friend on his shoulder, Moshe ran away from them, further down the road leading out of Frankfurt-am-Main. But how long could he continue running this way? Flushed and out of breath, Moshe neared some outlying houses. He panted spasmodically and realized that he could no longer keep ahead of his pursuers.

"Moshe! Moshe!" a woman's voice called from a yard. When the woman came up to him and kissed him on the head, Moshe protested furiously. But the woman interrupted him, "Have you forgotten me, Moshe dear? When you were a baby, I was your nursemaid, and I still remember you." She brought Moshe and his friend into her house until the ruffians were gone.

Then Moshe set out on his way again.

Evening came. Rabbi Adler's carriage rolled up before a roadside inn. "We'll spend the night here!" the coachman sang out. "Please go inside, and I'll put the horses in the stable and bring in the luggage!"

Rabbi Adler opened the door and stepped into the inn. Did the candlelights deceive his eyes? "Moshe? You? You must have travelled here by a miracle!"

Answering the look in Moshe's eyes, Rabbi Adler added, "If so, Moshe, you may come with me to Boskowitz."

Although Moshe had not planned it, he was never again to return to Frankfurt-am-Main except for brief visits. Nevertheless, for the rest of his life, Frankfurt-am-Main remained a powerful influence on him. He always signed his letters, "the insignificant Moshe Sofer from Frankfurt-am-Main."

In addition, he always celebrated Frankfurt-am-Main's *Purim Vincenz* on the twentieth of *Adar*, which celebrated the restoration of the Jewish community in 1614. (However, in order to obviate any doubts about the need for him to celebrate, he would always conclude a tractate of Talmud in order that the meal be considered a festive meal.) And in his letters and response, he often cited many things that he had seen and heard regarding custom and *halachah*.

On the way to Boskowitz, Rabbi Adler and Moshe passed through the city of Prague. There, Rabbi Yechezkel Landau, author of the *Noda Biyehudah* and Chief Rabbi of the city,[1] invited Rabbi Adler to give a talk to the congregation on *Shabbos*.

At one point, Rabbi Landau and Rabbi Adler engaged in an argument over the interpretation of a statement of the Ravad (a commentator on the Talmud), using Moshe as a go-between to deliver their messages to each other. In this debate, Rabbi Adler persuaded Rabbi Landau to retract his opinion.

But more remarkable was Moshe's approaching Rabbi Landau, who was then a quite venerable seventy-two-year-old

---

[1]See The *Noda Biyehudah* by Rabbi R. Weingarten, CIS, New Jersey, 1991.

Torah-leader, and providing him with the answer to a question that he had raised in one of his response. Rabbi Landau was pleased with the young man's response, and he exclaimed, "Excellent!"

In Boskowitz itself, a town of three hundred Jewish families, Moshe learned *Shulchan Aruch* with Rabbi Shmuel Kellin, author of *Machatzis Hashekel*. With Rabbi Adler, Moshe learned both Talmud and *Kabbalah*. Rabbi Adler taught Moshe not only theoretical but practical *Kabbalah* as well. In later years, Rabbi Moshe Sofer reflected, "Holy names have actual power, as I saw with my own eyes when they were used by the man of miracles, my teacher, Rabbi Adler."

But the murmuring began in Boskowitz as well. "All Jews are holy. What right does this Rabbi Adler have to enter our community and act more piously than anyone else? What right does he have to be so stringent about the laws of slaughtering?" Some people went so far as to denounce him to the gentile authorities.

At one time, someone informed an official that Rabbi Adler was illegally hoarding silver, despite the government's decree that all silver must be given to the state. This referred to the silver rings on Rabbi Adler's Torah scroll, which he had a right to own, since it was being used for a religious purpose.

Government officials came to the house to seize the Torah scroll. Rabbi Adler hastily took the scroll before they could enter and put it into Moshe's hand.

"Stand there in the middle of the room and do not move!" he commanded. Moshe stood stock-still as the officials searched throughout the house, unaware of Moshe's presence. Rabbi Adler had made him, for all intents and purposes, invisible.

In later years, Rabbi Moshe Sofer said that one should not be surprised that Rabbi Adler had the power to do this. However, Rabbi Sofer added, it is a very dangerous thing to attempt.

Another evening, as Rabbi Adler and Moshe sat learning, they heard a noise in the attic. Rabbi Adler told Moshe to go up and investigate. Although Moshe was frightened to do so, he had to obey his teacher.

There in the dark attic, Moshe saw a white-bearded Jew banging away at the Torah scroll with his stick. The Jew looked up, and Moshe was astonished.

"Rabbi Kellin! What are you doing here?"

"Moshe! You frightened me. Do not tell Rabbi Adler that I am here. I am taking the silver rings off his Torah scroll. Someone has informed on him, and soldiers might come into the house to seize the scroll. But don't let him know that people have been evil enough to inform on him."

Another time, Rabbi Adler had to flee Boskowitz due to an informer. When they left Boskowitz, the wagon driver fell asleep, and he opened his eyes two hours later to find that they had already arrived in Vienna. The wagon driver was astounded at this miraculous flight.

At the height of Rabbi Adler's persecution, Moshe asked him, "Rabbi, how can it be that although you are such a holy man, these people attack you and are not punished?"

Rabbi Adler replied, "Don't worry, my son. You will see that in the future every single one of them will become impoverished and will come knocking at your door for help."

In addition to this persecution, Rabbi Adler suffered personal tragedy. He had a small son and a twelve-year-old daughter whom Rabbi Sofer described in later years as "pleasing in her actions" and "beyond praise." This daughter died while they were in Boskowitz. Rabbi Sofer went on to tell, "Rabbi Nassan did not cry out, but he justified G-d's decree to himself with great joy, the like of which I never saw. On *Shabbos Parshas Vayeira*, when he was in mourning, he nevertheless followed his usual custom of going to the Torah as *kohein* and again as *maftir*. When he was reciting the *haftorah*, a tear fell from his eye. (This *haftorah* describes the death of the son of the woman of *Shunem*, whom the prophet Elisha supernaturally restored to life.) He let the tear fall into his hand, and he immediately turned into a new man, and again showed absolutely no sign of mourning, and he did not mention the girl's name at all (throughout the *Shabbos*)."

In this letter, Rabbi Sofer added, "Rabbi Adler had no more children, and made no effort to seek children from G-d. I believe that his wife was too old to have children, and he didn't want to force Heaven to create a miracle for him, because he was afraid that this might harm his wife."

Although Rabbi Adler had enemies among the people of Boskowitz, they were pleased with his student, Moshe. They used to say, "One visitor from Germany—meaning, Rabbi Adler—came here to bring us the other German—meaning, Moshe."

This was typical of Moshe's future career. Among Torah-observant Jews, Rabbi Moshe Sofer was never a subject of controversy. He grew to be a man whom all the people, learned and laymen, *chassidic* and non-*chassidic*, looked to as someone who expressed the voice of Torah.

Finally, after three years of controversy, Rabbi Adler could take no more. If Frankfurt-am-Main had been bad, Boskowitz was ten times worse. He decided to return home.

In 1786, Rabbi Adler left Boskowitz, accompanied by his student, Moshe, like the wandering ark accompanied by the *kohanim*.

10

Seeds of Reform

AN OIL PORTRAIT HUNG UPON THE WALL. HEAVY, WHITE CURTAINS were draped about the large, window looking out across the street at a mansion behind a manicured lawn. Next to the thick, quilt-covered bed, a throw rug covered the parquet floor.

Moshe stood up from the high-backed chair at the escritoire, where he had been writing notes in the margin of his *Gemara*. Through the window, he saw a white and scarlet carriage with an escutcheon on its side pull up before the opposite mansion. The gloved and uniformed chauffeur leaped down from his perch to open the little door for a regal banker, whom he helped step down. A butler stepped out of the mansion and nimbly hurried down the marble stairs to escort the man to the house.

Moshe turned away from the window. So this was Vienna!

He had not dreamed that his journey home from Boskowitz would bring him to the home of a member of the famous Arnstein family.

Nassan Arnstein was a wealthy businessman who dealt with banks and governments. When Rabbi Adler and Moshe Sofer had come to Vienna, Nassan Arnstein had invited them to stay at his house. This was considered a prestigious honor.

Moshe passed out of the room, through an elegant corridor studded with lamp-holders, passing the library with its thousands of handsomely-bound volumes.

Opening a broad, white double-door, Moshe stepped into the parlor.

"A little shorter by my ear, please, Pierre."

"Madame."

A man holding a pair of scissors raised in his hand was bending over a white-gowned woman who sat on a chair. The chair sat upon a large sheet, on which curled locks of her black hair lay.

Moshe tread forward. The barber moved to the side, and Moshe's eyes met those of Nassan Arnstein's daughter-in-law.

"How can you have a man cut your hair?" Moshe burst forth.

The woman stood up from the chair, her eyes flashing and her lips trembling with rage. "What are you saying?"

"You are a Jewish daughter and a married woman," Moshe continued. "This is not modest behavior."

The woman angrily spat at him, "I will not have a *yeshivah* student come into my house and tell me what to do. Times are changing, young man. You clerics no longer rule over us with your piddling regulations. Go back to your medieval ghetto. As for me, I will be a Jewess and a civilized European as well." She sat back down in her chair. "Continue, Pierre."

His face burning with anger and shame, Moshe hurried out of the room.

That evening, Nassan Arnstein summoned Moshe and Rabbi Adler to him in the library.

"Brandy?" he asked them sociably. "No? Well, I hope you don't mind if I have a little. It's been a long day." He poured himself a glass and toasted them. *Lechaim!*"

Nassan Arnstein swirled the wine glass and brought it to his lips. "Ahhh. Quite excellent." He set the glass down. "Now, gentlemen. I am afraid I must allude to a delicate affair. My daughter-in-law is quite high-strung, you know, quite emotional. You know how women are. After the little contretemps she had this afternoon with this young man, she has taken it into her head to insist that she will leave my house and return to her parents unless I accede to her wishes.

"Of course, Rabbi Adler, I am the first to admit that my daughter-in-law's indiscretion was not correct. And young man, I am glad that you rebuked her. But you know, it is so glamorous nowadays to be swayed by these heady new speeches of emancipation and rational thinking that the young find so fascinating. I am sure that my daughter-in-law will soon tire of these passing fads. In the meantime, though, gentlemen, for the sake of peace within my own household, I am afraid that I must most regretfully ask you to seek lodging elsewhere. I hope you understand, as men of the world, that sometimes we must bend over backwards to humor our little women . . ."

As the two men left the house of the Arnsteins, Moshe reflected on the many signs he had seen in cosmopolitan Vienna of changes in Torah-observant Jews. All these changes seemed to be driven by a desire to break out of exile, to break out of poverty, to break out of the intellectual imprisonment and to enter the exciting world of the gentile European community. This community was now rising up from the tyrannies of a thousand years and speaking fervently of concepts such as freedom, liberty and an end to poverty and religious persecution. It seemed that many Jews who were excited by these ideas felt that to join this exhilarating movement, they must start to set aside their Judaism.

Three years earlier, in 1783, soon after Rabbi Adler and Moshe Sofer had gone to Boskowitz, a controversial book had burst upon the Jewish scene—Moses Mendelssohn's translation of the *Chumash* into German, accompanied by a *Biur*, or commentary, based on classical sources of *peshat*, or the simple meaning of the text.

The book swept across Europe. Some rabbis praised it; others vigorously denounced it. In Frankfurt-am-Main, Rabbi Horowitz gave an impassioned and eloquent speech censuring the work. In many communities, the volume was banned, yet *yeshivah* students surreptitiously read the forbidden literature in frightened and excited secrecy.

What was the power, the attraction and the danger, that people saw in this volume?

One cannot understand or judge this work in itself. Rather, one must see it within the context of the times, and in particular of the burgeoning *Haskalah* movement, of which Moses Mendelssohn was a prime spokesman and mover.

The *Haskalah* was the Jewish reflection of the gentile Enlightenment of the eighteenth century. The proponents of this new movement believed that Torah Judaism had been stifled and crushed by the experience of Jews in the cruel and ruthless exile.

But now, gentiles were beginning to arise and speak out bravely against the cruelties and violence of the church and governments. These gentiles were proposing ideas of freedom instead of servitude; liberty instead of persecution; science in place of ignorance; and reason in place of superstition. These ideas were the light—the Enlightenment—that they hoped would not only redeem Europe, but illuminate the eyes of Jews as well.

Moses Mendelssohn was the symbol of joining Judaism to the Enlightenment. Born in 1729 in Dessau, he himself was the son of a scribe, a *sofer*. After a childhood steeped in Talmud studies, Mendelssohn was attracted to classical Torah philosophical studies. Soon afterwards, he went to Berlin and immersed himself in secular learning. So extreme was his desire for knowledge that his ruthless learning schedule ruined his health and made him into a hunchback.

In 1750, Mendelssohn gained fame for his written defense of a play entitled *The Jews* by the German playwright Gotthold Ephraim Lessing. This was the first play in Christian history to portray a Jew as noble and unselfish. As a result, it was severely attacked. "It is not impossible, but certainly highly improbable," wrote one respected critic, "that such a noble spirit could form itself. The improbability obstructs our pleasure. Even a modicum of virtue and honesty is so seldom found among this nation that the few instances thereof do not dispel our detestation."

In his reply, Mendelssohn wrote passionately, "What a humiliation for our oppressed nation. What excessive contempt! The common people among the Christians have from time immemorial regarded us as the scum of creation, as sores upon human society. But I have always assumed that cultivated people held a fairer opinion."

After this, Mendelssohn wrote a series of philosophical writings in German that won the highest praise, and he became friendly with the greatest intellectual leaders of Europe, in particular, Immanuel Kant.

By the mid-1700s, when Moshe Sofer was an infant in Frankfurt-am-Main, Mendelssohn had gained the sobriquet, "the German Plato," and his house was a salon where the intellectual aristocrats of Berlin would gather.

His initial humanistic, philosophical writings had nothing to do with Judaism. But now, as the result of challenges to his faith, Mendelssohn began to defend Judaism to the gentile world, and he became an active fighter in the struggle for the Jews' civil rights. In addition, he began to formulate his own vision of what Judaism meant and should mean, and he began to make practical moves to further his ideals.

Mendelssohn wished to reconcile Torah with the rationalism of his time. "Faith," he wrote, "accepts no commands. It accepts only what comes to it by way of reasoned conviction." Elsewhere, he wrote, "I do not understand what could possibly bind me to this seemingly overstrict and generally despised religion, if I were not convinced in my heart of its truth."

Therefore, when faced with a conflict between the philosophy of emancipation and the rules of Torah, Mendelssohn faced a dilemma. He wished to see Judaism solely as a religion based on reason. He did not believe that Judaism had the right to impose its views or community standards. Whether or not to observe *mitzvos* or to believe in the principles of Jewish faith, he said, was up to the individual. He added, "Let every man who does not disturb the public welfare, who obeys the law, acts righteously towards you and his fellow man be allowed to speak as he thinks, to pray to G-d after his own fashion or after that of his fathers, and to seek eternal salvation where he thinks he may find it."

This was a retreat from Torah and a plea for natural religion and natural ethics. Such a doctrine could only spin itself out to its logical conclusion of denial of faith in a specifically Jewish allegiance to G-d. Although viewing Torah as ideally true, Mendelssohn believed that it had been corrupted in practice. "I shall not deny that I have detected in my religion human increments and abuses that, unfortunately, must obscure its radiance. What friend of truth can boast of having found his religion free of harmful human additives? We all know this poisonous breath of hypocrisy and superstition, and those of us who are seekers of the truth wish that we might purge the poison without harming the good."

Such words of powerful rebuke had been spoken to the Jewish people since the times of the prophets. But there was a crucial difference, and that was the solution proposed to correct the problem. The prophets and all subsequent leaders of the Jews had urged the Jews to ameliorate their problems through greater adherence to Torah and ethical behavior. Mendelssohn, blinded by the light of the Enlightenment, urged them to improve themselves through access to non-Jewish refinement and culture. Jews had to be brought in touch with the new, enlightened culture, whose ideals of equality and brotherhood were gradually overcoming the deep and ingrained hatred and cruelty of the gentile past.

Mendelssohn believed that the Jews had, as a despised people, been forced to cling to Torah as an alternative to the refining and enlightening culture that he saw in his intellectual circle. Indeed, he wrote, "My nation has been kept at such a distance from culture that one might almost doubt the possibility of improvement."

Mendelssohn honored German culture and the German language in particular. Once, he went so far as to court disaster by criticizing King Frederick the Great for writing poetry in French, and thus abandoning the German language. "Will the Germans never be aware of their own value?" he wrote. "Will they forever exchange their gold [their thought] for their neighbors' tinsel [French literature]?"

Mendelssohn wanted to draw Jews to this European, and specifically German, culture. He wished to take them away from their Yiddish, which in his mind was a barbarous pidgin, an ugly jargon grotesquely mimicking the stately and beautiful sonority of German.

But how could he accomplish his aims when the Jews clung so stubbornly to their "backward" way of life? The answer was to utilize the Torah to which the Jews owed their loyalty.

Mendelssohn turned from addressing the non-Jews of Germany and addressed himself to changing the Jewish condition. He printed the *Chumash* accompanied by a translation in a literary German that was printed in Hebrew characters, along with his *Biur*. The *Biur* was solely concerned with analyzing the simple meaning of the text and the grammatical issues involved. No reference was made to rabbinic interpretations.

The purpose of the translation was not to bring the *Chumash* to those who spoke German. Rather, it was to serve as a means of teaching literary German to those who knew only Yiddish.

In addition, the commentary was written with an ulterior motive. Commentaries based on the simple meaning of the text and involved in questions of grammar were not new. Such works had been written by great Torah authorities such as the Rashbam and Avraham Ibn Ezra. But the intent of those commentaries was to teach the simple meaning of the words before one looked at them in the light of the *Midrash*. The *Biur's* intent was to devalue the traditional approach of the sages of the Talmud and *Midrash*.

As a result, when this volume appeared, it aroused a great storm. In many places, the work was wildly successful. It was widely read not only in Germany, but in Holland, Denmark, England and France, as well. As Mendelssohn had hoped, his work proved to be the crack in the door that brought the German language and European culture into the Jewish ghettos.

Torah leaders, however, realized immediately that this work posed a threat to the traditional way of Jewish life. The work was proclaimed heretical, and its study forbidden under threat of excommunication.

When Mendelssohn died in 1786, his disciples eulogized him, "Truth and the authentic interpretation of the Torah were obscured in darkness for generations, until G-d commanded, 'Let Moses appear,' and at once there was light." Only a few years were to pass, however, before this movement plunged its adherents into darkness with mass abandonment of Torah and conversion to Christianity.

With dizzying rapidity, the attempt of the "Berlin *Haskalah*," as it was called, to update Judaism led to complete assimilation. (The much later Russian *Haskalah*, while leading to abandonment of Torah, did not lead to such a great extent to an abdication of Jewish identity and widespread apostasy.)

The members of the Berlin *Haskalah* first distanced themselves from the East European Jew, who was so distinctively different than the non-Jew. They distanced themselves from the "jargon," Yiddish. But they soon outpaced Mendelssohn, who had to the end of his days professed being a Torah-observant Jew.

Mendelssohn's followers took his adherence to the doctrine of rationalism seriously . He believed in Torah but reduced it to a rational creed. But the Torah has many seemingly irrational elements. To loyally keep the apparently irrational laws of a religion, while professing that all religion must be rational could not continue for long.

Soon his followers gave up belief in the coming of the *Mashiach* and in the unity of the Jewish people.

But even at this point, the members of the Berlin *Haskalah* found themselves frustrated, for all their efforts still did not suffice to gain them entrance to gentile culture. No matter how much they became more modern and enlightened, they were not able to gain the agreement of the Christian states to cease persecuting the Jews and to give the Jews equal civil and legal rights. It was not assimilation that the Christians desired;

it was conversion. And so the movement triggered by a Torah-observant Jew resulted in an epidemic of conversions to Christianity. In the words of Heinrich Graetz, a 19th century Jewish historian and *Haskalah* disciple, "They were like moths, fluttering around the flame, until they were consumed."

Mendelssohn's own children and grandchildren converted to Christianity. His daughter, Dorothea, abandoned her husband for a German intellectual and then became a Lutheran. Another daughter, Henrietta, passionately embraced Catholicism. With one exception, all of Mendelssohn's sons also became Christians.

Mendelssohn's daring experiment based on his belief in the new spirit of the day had evolved into disaster.

And in the atmosphere of sophisticated Vienna, Moshe Sofer saw first-hand the first impressions that Haskalah was making on Jews.

11

As a Young Teacher

IN THE SAME YEAR THAT MENDELSSOHN DIED AND HIS ADHERENTS began spreading his tenets, Rabbi Moshe Sofer finished his apprenticeship as a student and began the next phase in his life as a teacher and leader. And it was as a leader that he battled against the corrosive influence of those who, in the name of Enlightenment, attempted to destroy the adherence of the Jews to the Torah.

Rabbi Adler and his student Moshe left Vienna and continued on their journey back to Frankfurt-am-Main. It was perhaps during this journey that the following episode took place.

The breath steamed from the horses' nostrils and swiftly vanished into the frosty air. Their hooves clopped against the beaten, icy snow. The road stretched before and after the slowly-moving carriage, surrounded by broad expanses of snowy fields and occasional trees whose branches sagged under their gentle white burden.

The pale sun had risen high into the sky. Inside the carriage, Rabbi Adler and Moshe sat beneath a blanket in the chilly air. Moshe saw Rabbi Adler glance at the bundle of food they had brought along, and then gaze out the small carriage window.

"It's too cold to sit," Moshe said. "I'm going to go out and walk alongside the carriage to warm up."

Rabbi Adler nodded. As Moshe stepped out of the slowly-moving carriage, he surreptitiously took hold of Rabbi Adler's cup that he used to wash his hands with.

Walking alongside the carriage on the icy road, Moshe bent over and took a handful of snow. He squeezed the snow over the cup so that the warmth of his hand melted the snow. He did this a number of times until his hand was numb with the cold and the cup was filled with water.

Holding the cup steady, Moshe carefully opened the door of the moving carriage and stepped back inside. Moshe handed the cup to Rabbi Adler. "I brought you water to wash your hands."

Rabbi Adler's face lit up. "You are a true student!" he exclaimed with delight.

(It is possible that this episode took place earlier, because in later years Rabbi Moshe Sofer related, "With my little hands I melted snow for my rabbi," which may imply that he was a youngster at the time.)

The carriage rolled into the town of Fuerth, Bavaria. Rabbi Adler and Moshe stayed there overnight, and the next morning, Moshe was up early to accompany his rabbi.

Rabbi Adler turned away from the window that looked onto the snowy alley. "I am continuing on to Frankfurt-am-Main," he said. "But the time has come for us to go on separate ways."

Moshe's eyes widened. "But Rabbi—"

"You are twenty-three years old. The time has come for you to reach your own stature. You are no longer a student, Moshe."

"Don't ask me to leave you!"

"I am afraid I must push the fledgling out of the nest, Moshe. This is the way of Torah. As long as Yitzchak remained with Avraham, G-d's spirit didn't rest upon him. As long as Yaakov remained with Yitzchak, and as long as Yehoshua remained with Moshe, G-d's spirit didn't rest upon them. Only when the student leaves his teacher can he achieve his own greatness. Now it is your turn as well, Moshe."

"But where will I go?" cried Moshe.

"I want you to go to Prossnitz."

"Prossnitz? But Rabbi, Prossnitz is a town without a rabbi, without an *av beis din*. And there is a group of the followers of Shabbesai Tzvi!"

"Nevertheless."

Moshe did not protest further. This was the will of his *rebbe*, and he would follow his *rebbe's* wishes to the end.

That morning, two carriages left Fuerth. They travelled together down a narrow road and then, at a crossroads close outside the town, one of the carriages turned left and the other turned right. Rabbi Moshe Sofer was now on his own.

When Rabbi Adler returned to Frankfurt-am-Main, he was greeted by his friends and admirers. He again established his *yeshivah* and his private *minyan*. The leaders of the community said nothing, thinking that it was better not to create a controversy with such a holy man.

As for Moshe, immediately upon his arrival in Prossnitz, students approached him to learn with him, and he also taught laymen. This beginning of his career was typical, for he always saw himself as principally a teacher of Torah. In a letter that he wrote in later years, Rabbi Sofer said, "From the year

5546 (1785/6) and onwards, I have been a teacher. As for everything else, I do it only because it is necessary, like someone walking on hot coals."

12

Looking for a Wife

"FATHER, WHY DID YOU WAIT SO LONG TO GET MARRIED?"

In later years, when Rabbi Moshe Sofer was an older man, his son, Rabbi Shimon Sofer, Chief Rabbi of Cracow, put this question to him. "Weren't you concerned with our sages' statement that 'a person should get married at age eighteen'?"

Rabbi Sofer sighed. "Yes, my son. I know this very well. But I was in poor health. Every month I needed a bloodletting because of my sicknesses. I have had recurrences ever since, for my health has always been precarious."

In his first year at Prossnitz, Rabbi Sofer received a letter from Rabbi Shmuel Kellin, the author of *Machatzis Hashekel*, who had been one of his teachers in Boskowitz. A wealthy and respectable man from Nikolsburg had approached Rabbi Kellin, seeking an outstanding Torah student for his daughter. The man had promised a substantial dowry.

Rabbi Sofer agreed to go see the man and went to Nikolsburg to spend *Shabbos* there. His visit was anticipated by the scholars there, because he had already gained a fine reputation. He engaged in Torah conversation with them, and they were impressed.

Towards evening, after *Minchah*, the wealthy father and Rabbi Sofer went for a stroll to talk matters over.

"Don't worry about making a living," the man informed Rabbi Sofer. "After you get married, I will support you for a few years, and then I have a rabbinical post for you in a good community. Mmm? What do you say?"

"I, um, excuse me. I have to think things over."

Rabbinical post? Rabbi Sofer didn't want to be a public figure. The life of a communal rabbi was not his own. He had to deal with women bringing chickens to ask if they were kosher; he had to deal with government decrees; he had to deal with arguments, with politics, with maneuverings, with budgets and distribution of funds. Those who were strict would claim he was not serious; those who were lenient would claim he was too harsh. Those who had wealth would attempt to control him; those who had power would try to intimidate him. Rabbi Sofer wanted merely to sit with his holy books and in his solitude be close to G-d. Only when freed from the petty concerns of this worldly life could he develop himself. Only when he was removed from the vanities of the world could he spread Torah in its purity.

Rabbi Sofer strode away. The rest of that *Shabbos*, and until he left Nikolsburg, Rabbi Sofer avoided the man. He had nothing more to say to him. He would not be dragged into such a match. He would not be taken away from his learning. This man, who meant so much good, had no idea how much pain it caused Rabbi Sofer to be threatened with the loss of his clinging to Torah.

"You have to be realistic!" people would say. "You have to

compromise with the world. You have to earn a living and support a family. The Talmud says that you have to combine Torah with a craft. And after all, you can still be a rabbi."

People meant well. But no one could see into Rabbi Sofer's heart. No one could see that for him there was only one definition of life, and that was the life of Torah. For him, there was only one definition of the world, and that was the world of serving G-d. What good would it do him to be reasonable, to compromise, to accommodate? What that really meant was to give up his fiery attachment to Torah and to lay his soul to rest. He would come to life in this world and people would say that he was living a normal life, a communal rabbi raising a family. But under such conditions that forced him to give up much of his time for Torah learning, would he really have a meaningful life?

No! He would not compromise. Rabbi Kellin meant well, but he could not agree to such a match. Even to speak of it, even to expend words defending his position was to give it too much energy.

The next day, without seeing the man again, Rabbi Sofer hired a carriage to bring him back to Boskowitz.

When Rabbi Sofer entered the familiar *beis midrash*, Rabbi Kellin looked up at him from his learning. "*Mazel tov!*"

Rabbi Sofer shook his head. "I am not engaged."

"What! Not engaged? What went wrong?"

"The man wanted me to become a community rabbi."

"A community rabbi? And what's wrong with that?"

Rabbi Sofer remained silent.

"Listen to me," Rabbi Kellin said excitedly. "You cannot get away from it. I say that you shall become a community rabbi, and indeed you shall become a community rabbi!"

Perhaps Rabbi Sofer thought in his heart that Rabbi Kellin's words were unfair, for Rabbi Kellin had often declined prestigious rabbinical positions, preferring the life of a small-town teacher. Once, Rabbi Kellin had received a letter from the elders of Pressburg inviting him to become their chief rabbi. Rabbi Kellin had written back a letter saying that he was not fit for the post. However, he added, if they would accept him, he would agree to become the *shul-klapper* (the person who knocks on the windows of the houses to awaken people for *davening*).

In later years, when Rabbi Sofer would tell this story to his students, he would sigh and exclaim, "How great is the curse of a righteous man. Because of this statement, I was ultimately forced to accept a rabbinical post."

But at this point, such a compromise was out of the question in Rabbi Sofer's mind. Still clinging to his principles, he took leave of Rabbi Kellin and returned to Prossnitz.

At that time, Rabbi Kellin's son, Rabbi Wolf Kellin, was appointed *av beis din* of Prossnitz. Rabbi Kellin wrote him, "My son, when you come to Prossnitz and find there the young man from Frankfurt (as Rabbi Sofer was called), do not stray from anything he tells you."

The two young men met and became fast friends. They both taught Torah, and the students of Rabbi Wolf Kellin also went to learn with Rabbi Sofer.

13

Marriage and Opposition

"THOUGH I AM HER BROTHER, AND I AM PREJUDICE, EVERYONE WILL tell you that my sister Sarah is a fine and worthy daughter of Israel," Rabbi Hirsch Yerwitz said. "She is modest and charitable, and the daughter of a Torah sage. Our father was the much-loved and revered *rav* of this town until his untimely passing. There can be no question about her fine family background."

Rabbi Sofer said nothing.

"As for practical matters," Rabbi Yerwitz continued, "I am, thank G-d, well-off. After the wedding, I will support you for four years. You will be able to sit and learn Torah without any distractions. *Nu*, can there be anything more to say?"

Rabbi Sofer remained silent a moment. In fact, there was something else to say. The intended bride, Sarah, was a few years older than him. But this was a secondary matter. Now he would be able to learn Torah in undisturbed sanctity, without any constraining commitments.

Rabbi Sofer put out his hand.

Rabbi Yerwitz shook it warmly. *"Mazel tov!"*

Soon after, in 5625 (1786), the engagement contract was signed. Now it was time for Rabbi Sofer to return to Frankfurt-am-Main and receive his mother's blessing.

Rabbi Sofer's mother looked up at the handsome young man who came into her room. He was tall and slender, with dark eyes and a full, dark beard. On his head, he wore a soft, fur hat, and he wore an impeccable caftan. Many years ago, a boy had left Frankfurt-am-Main. Now a handsome and confident young man with intense eyes and sensitive expression had returned.

"Mother!" Rabbi Sofer exclaimed.

Tears came to her eyes and coursed down her pale, lined cheeks.

"Moshe, I am so glad that you have come." She wiped away her tears with a small hand, framed at the wrist with cambric lace.

They sat comfortably together and discussed old times, and Rabbi Sofer told of his life in the intervening years.

"Ah, Moshe," his mother said, "I shall be glad when you return to Frankfurt-am-Main and get married here."

"What do you mean, Mother?"

"What do I mean? You surprise me, Moshe. I mean that like all young people do, you have gone off on your own and you have changed from being a boy to being a man. I am a widow, Moshe, and you are my oldest child. I will be very glad when you return home."

Moshe was in a quandary. Return home to Frankfurt-am-Main and get married here? He had already signed an engagement contract in Prossnitz, agreeing to live in his brother-in-law's house.

"Moshe, you are still so quiet. You must be tired after the long journey. Go to sleep. I made your bed for you."

Rabbi Sofer stood up heavily. "I will not go to bed yet. I have to *daven Maariv*."

As Rabbi Sofer walked to Rabbi Horowitz's *beis midrash*, the fresh air cleared his head. He would have to disappoint his mother. He had signed an agreement with his bride and he would not back out.

Through a storm of mixed emotions, Rabbi Sofer held to his resolve. Again, he greeted Rabbi Horowitz in the familiar *beis midrash*, *davened Maariv*, greeted old friends and saw new faces, and heard snatches of conversation and of Torah learning. He approached Rabbi Horowitz and asked to speak to him. They passed down the narrow corridor and entered Rabbi Horowitz's private study, where the candle on the desk cast shadows across Rabbi Horowitz's face.

"Your uncle has given me a thousand gulden to hold in trust," Rabbi Horowitz said in measured words. "As you know, your uncle's only son grew quite ill, and your uncle made a vow that he would give a third of this sum if his son recovered. Now his son has made a complete recovery. Let me ask you, what are your plans?"

"Well. I don't think I told you . . . I am engaged to a woman . . . in Prossnitz."

"Your mother did not tell me that."

"No, I . . . I didn't tell her yet."

"Do you know that your mother wants you to get married here in Frankfurt-am-Main?"

"Yes. She told me tonight, but I've already signed the engagement contract."

"She only told you tonight, and before this, you did not know?"

"The woman is the daughter of Rabbi Yerwitz and I saw no reason to delay."

83

"Where will you live, Moshe?"

"Why, in Prossnitz. I made an agreement that we would live in her brother's house—"

"But your mother wants you to marry here, Moshe."

"Yes, but I made an agreement—"

"You agreed in error, Moshe. They will understand. You did not know the wishes of your mother."

"But still . . . but even so . . . you know that Torah students here in Frankfurt-am-Main usually don't get married until they are thirty years old. I will not wait another seven years before I can find a wife."

"Your mother's wishes, Moshe."

"But must I wait seven more years?"

"Your mother's wishes, Moshe. And if you will not agree, I shall continue to hold in trust the gulden that your uncle put in my hands."

"Will not agree? I *cannot* agree! Heaven knows I cannot wait seven more years."

With this unpleasant exchange, Rabbi Sofer's interview with his teacher Rabbi Horowitz drew to an end.

Rabbi Sofer's meeting with his great *rebbe*, his teacher in all matters, his guide and mentor, was no less distressing.

"She is older than you, Moshe," Rabbi Adler discouraged him. "Give her up. You have made a mistaken agreement. There is a young woman here in Frankfurt-am-Main of a wealthy and respected family. We have spoken of you already. They are favorably inclined."

"But it wasn't a mistaken agreement."

"You did not understand what you were agreeing to. A woman so much older than you, Moshe. Will she bear you children?"

Rabbi Sofer held stubbornly to his position. He had made a decision; he had made a commitment. He was not going back on his word.

"Indeed," Rabbi Adler mused. "I sent you from me to become more independent . . ."

A few days later, Rabbi Sofer was riding in a bumpy carriage back to Prossnitz. His mother had been tearful, and Rabbi Sofer had comforted her as best he could. Rabbi Horowitz had not relented and still held the money. (As it happened, Rabbi Sofer's uncle later grew poor. Rabbi Sofer lent him the money that Rabbi Horowitz was holding, and never got it back.)

Rabbi Sofer had made a decision and he was convinced that it was right. He could not back out of it, for that would be immoral. Even if it hurt his mother; even if his own rabbis, giants of the generation, dissuaded him, he would not be swayed. Hard inside as steel, he was going back to Prossnitz and meeting the dictates of his will and conscience.

But after Rabbi Sofer returned to Prossnitz, conditions drastically changed.

In the Austrian Empire Jews were subject to the whims of the landed nobility, the magnates. These magnates gave Jews the Charters of Privilege allowing them to settle in certain areas. These charters of privilege set out the Jews' obligations, and the rights and protection to which they were entitled.

Without such a permit, Jews were not allowed to settle in a town. In many areas, Jews were not allowed to live at all. This was true of many of the large cities. For many years, for instance, Jews had been banished from Pressburg and Buda. Jews were largely confined to towns and villages, or forced to wander through the countryside trying to earn a livelihood. Depending on the political winds, these rules could become stricter. And so it happened now.

The news passed through the town swiftly. A new law had been enacted for the region of Moravia, limiting the number of Jews who could get married per year. In addition, the law stated that no Jew born outside of Moravia was allowed to settle there permanently. The purpose of these laws was, of course, to limit the number of Jews living in Moravia.

As a non-citizen of Moravia, Rabbi Sofer had neither the right to get married nor to continue to live in Prossnitz for any length of time.

Now he was at an impasse. He had gotten engaged on the understanding that he would live in his brother-in-law's house and be supported while he learned Torah. But now, this new decree meant that he would have to leave Prossnitz without any means of support.

Until now, Rabbi Sofer had defied the wishes of his mother and his teachers in order to honor the pledge that he had made to his fiancee. But now she was seemingly unable to fulfill her obligations to him. Perhaps, therefore, his obligation to her was dissolved. Perhaps he should follow the wishes of those who had urged him to return to Frankfurt-am-Main and marry someone else, someone younger and more seemingly suited for him.

Rabbi Sofer sat down and penned a letter to Rabbi Horowitz. He described the situation and asked Rabbi Horowitz whether in light of these new circumstances he should break off his engagement.

Three months passed, and there was no answer but silence. What was the meaning of this? Rabbi Sofer considered that Rabbi Horowitz was not answering because he did not want to take responsibility for such a decision on his own shoulders.

Rabbi Sofer concluded that this was a decision that he would have to make on his own, without sharing the burden of the responsibility with anyone else.

He proceeded with the wedding plans.

On *Lag B'omer* of 5547, (1787), when Rabbi Sofer was twenty-four years old, he and his bride stood under a *chuppah* in the town of Semnitz. They had traveled to Semnitz, which was just outside the border of Moravia, in order to circumvent the prohibition against marrying.

A few days later, a letter arrived for Rabbi Sofer. It was Rabbi Horowitz's reply to his request for advice. Rabbi Horowitz had responded immediately to Rabbi Sofer's letter. He wrote that Rabbi Sofer had a clear right to cancel the engagement, and he urged Rabbi Sofer to return to Frankfurt-am-Main, where he would be given a warm reception.

The letter had gotten side-tracked, and only now had it reached Rabbi Sofer—a few days too late!

But Rabbi Sofer was not disturbed. To the contrary, he saw the fact that the letter had been delayed a sign that despite the misgivings of Rabbi Horowitz, this was a marriage desired by Heaven.

Rabbi Sofer stayed in Semnitz, because he could not return to Prossnitz.

Meanwhile, the governmental decree was causing problems for Rabbi Wolf Kellin, the *av beis din* of Prossnitz and friend of Rabbi Sofer (also known as Rabbi Wolf Boskowitz). Because Rabbi Wolf Kellin had left the district of Moravia for a while, he had lost his rights as a citizen. The government had now decreed that in accordance with its new policy, he must leave Moravia.

The Jews of Prossnitz were in an uproar. The community leaders met and concluded that they would make a special petition to the Emperor, asking him to allow Rabbi Kellin to remain because, first of all, he had been born in Moravia and, secondly, because he was the *av beis din* of Prossnitz.

After this petition was circulated and signed, one of the men stood up and declared, "Since we are already submitting a petition to the Kaiser, let us add the request that Rabbi Moshe Sofer also be allowed to stay here." A few lines were appended describing Rabbi Sofer as a young man who had been living in Prossnitz for some years, teaching Torah as a public service, and asking that he be allowed to continue to stay.

An answer to the petition was soon forthcoming. Rabbi Kellin was given permission to remain in Moravia for an additional three years, during which time he had to actively seek a rabbinical post elsewhere. As for Rabbi Sofer, he was given permission to remain without any conditions.

When the news reached Rabbi Sofer, he returned together with his wife to Prossnitz, and moved into his brother-in-law's house to devote himself to learning.

Rabbi Moshe Sofer had plunged into marriage as the Jews had plunged into the Red Sea, without any indication that the conditions he had been promised would be fulfilled. And now, circumstances had suddenly shifted, and he was granted all those things that so recently had seemed impossible.

14

Into the Eye of the Storm

IT WAS *MOTZEI SHABBOS*. RABBI SOFER SAT DOWN TO LEARN BY candlelight. Dawn came, and Rabbi Sofer still sat learning. Morning came and went, and the afternoon lengthened into evening. Rabbi Sofer still sat over his *sefarim*. Finally, after having learned for twenty-four hours straight without taking time to eat anything, Rabbi Sofer closed his *sefarim*. He *davened Maariv* and went to sleep until eleven at night.

Then he got up, had some cake and coffee, and sat down to learn. Again, he learned through the whole night and through the entire next day until Monday evening. He *davened Maariv*, had a light meal and again stayed up the entire night and slept the next day.

This was not a rare and extraordinary feat that Rabbi Sofer managed to perform. This was Rabbi Sofer's regular schedule during his first two years of marriage.

In addition to his learning and teaching, Rabbi Sofer engaged in other *mitzvos*, such as joining Prossnitz's *chevrah kaddisha*.

During all the years of his stay in Prossnitz, Rabbi Sofer did not eat meat. He was apparently not comfortable with the scrupulousness of the butchers.

During these days of Rabbi Sofer's complete dedication to learning, great events were taking place in the world at large.

Haskalah, whose effects Rabbi Sofer had glimpsed in his sojourn through Vienna, was merely one result of the spirit of Enlightenment that was sweeping through Europe. This movement eventually affected all areas of life: political, social, religious and scientific.

The French Revolution soon led to radical changes in the face of the entire European continent.

The Enlightenment was a reaction to the cruelty and selfishness of the ruling powers of the time, both political and religious. The Enlightenment promised a new era that would recognize the rights of all people, an era that would do away with persecution and superstition. The advocates of this new movement spoke fervently of freedom and science.

Men, they said, had no right to treat each other cruelly, to discriminate against each other. The old values that justified brutality in the name of creed must be eliminated. What right did Christians have to persecute Jews? None! For after all, were not Jews as good as Christians? If you pricked them, did they not bleed too? Nearly two thousand years of Christianity had permitted massive internal corruption. Now the time was ripe to eliminate this, and establish a rule based on reason, equal rights and freedom of thought.

The architects of the movement declared that the Jews must be made equal citizens. But on the other hand, Jews believed in a non-rational religion. Therefore, the architects of the Enlightenment advocated a sweeping reform of Jewish religious life. There must be no more persecution of Jews—but there must also no longer be Jews as they had existed until now. Rather, all people must be citizens, brothers in the new doctrines of tolerance.

Jews were thus faced with a bewildering challenge. On the one hand stood the old, repressive, anti-Semitic forces that persecuted them, but allowed them some measure of inner autonomy to continue leading Torah lives. On the other stood those who fought for their civil liberties and economic rights, but who also tried to woo them away from Torah.

In Europe, the spirit of the Enlightenment found explosive expression in the French Revolution of 1789 and the subsequent Declaration of the Rights of Man. But these new advocates of equality were largely influenced by anti-Semitism themselves, and it was only after much debate that, on September 27, 1791, Jews were granted privileges equal to those enjoyed by all other citizens. But Jews were to be granted rights only to the degree that they betrayed their Torah and their independent nationhood. In the words of the famous formula of Parisian deputy, Clermont-Tonerre, "Everything for the Jews as citizens; nothing as a nation."

The French Revolution with its glorious promises was followed by a Reign of Terror in the course of which all religions were outlawed and Judaism came under attack. Those who waved the pennant of liberation were ultimately as savage as those whom they had so vigorously decried.

After a series of political convulsions, France began to war against its neighboring countries under the leadership of General Napoleon Bonaparte. These wars, while meant for conquest, also carried with them the doctrines of the Enlightenment.

Over the course of the next twenty-five years, the French spread their ideas to surrounding countries, particularly to Holland, Italy and parts of Germany and Russia. There the

Jews were included, however reluctantly, in the new formula of human worth.

This period, lasting from 1789 to 1815, was a heady and hopeful period of emancipation.

But even earlier, Emperor Joseph II, who ruled over the Austrian Empire from 1780-1790, was implementing legislation colored by the Enlightenment philosophy.

Emperor Joseph II's program of "enlightened absolutism" led him to ameliorate some of the terrible conditions under which Jews had been forced to live. Particularly significant was his repeal of the ban on Jewish residence in cities. He announced his intention to allow Jews a general education and to allow them to study technical trades. A number of government-sponsored schools were opened in various parts of Austria, including Prossnitz, Mattersdorf and Pressburg. Although these schools taught secular studies to a degree, they did not directly threaten Torah learning. Still, this policy gave rise to a great dispute among the Jews themselves. What was the emperor's intent? Was it benign or harmful? Even such a Jew as Moses Mendelssohn was suspicious of Emperor Joseph II's motives. Indeed, his seeming largesse had as its purpose the assimilation of Jews into the gentile population. The negative aspects of Emperor Joseph II's program became clear when, in 1789, he announced his intention to draft Jewish children into the army.

This attempt failed, and it had the effect of making many Jews extremely suspicious of all plans imposed from the outside promising to emancipate the Jews and to allow them to live freely.

This period was one in which, in the general culture, the forces of Enlightenment grappled with conservative and reactionary forces. Particularly after Napoleon's defeat in 1814, the reactionary forces would experience a return to power. Meanwhile, Jews were dealing with the struggle for

Jewish civil rights and the battle over the form of traditional Jewish life.

It was in the 1790s that the Haskalah began to make wider inroads. In later years, Rabbi Sofer would refer to this time as the era when the agitation against Torah learning and traditional Torah observance began. The Haskalah was having an effect in the major cities of Berlin, Breslau and Frankfurt, as well as Prague and Vienna. The problems of assimilation and the loosening of the allegiance to Torah were even beginning to affect the smaller towns of Prossnitz, Dressnitz and Mattersdorf.

In 1790, Rabbi Sofer directly addressed the problems being caused by the Haskalah. In line with his concerns as an educator, Rabbi Sofer wrote an elegy mourning the Haskalah influence on how Jewish children were being taught. "These precious children are clever," Rabbi Sofer wrote, "but they speak foreign tongues."

But Jews had to deal not only with problems from gentile governments and new reformers who attempted to abrogate the Torah. Secret followers of Shabbesai Tzvi were still attempting to disseminate their form of subversion.

Rabbi Sofer was very sensitive to any traces of *Shabbatean* influence. At one time, he met a man who referred disparagingly to one of the works of Rabbi Yaakov Emden, the Yavetz, who was a zealous crusader against *Shabbatean* influence. From this man's words, Rabbi Sofer understood that he was a secret follower of Shabbesai Tzvi. Another time, during the recital of *Tikkun Chatzos*, Rabbi Sofer saw a man sitting, unmoved by the commemoration of the destruction of the Beis Hamikdash. Here again, Rabbi Sofer induced that the man was a follower of Shabbesai Tzvi.

In addition, Jews had to deal with the intractable problem of trouble-makers who bred conflict in the community. In 1790, for instance, a scurrilous pamphlet defaming Rabbi

Adler was published in Frankfurt-am-Main. This pamphlet, entitled *Ma'aseh Ta'atuim* (Peculiar Activities), was a collection of distortions and lies accusing Rabbi Adler of engaging in practices that contradicted traditional Jewish customs. Its scornful, mocking tone prefigured the tone of derision that marked much of the Haskalah literature that denounced Jewish life and Torah traditions.

Unruffled in the eye of the hurricane, Rabbi Moshe Sofer learned in tranquility. But the center of the storm would not long remain peaceful. He was soon forced to step into the public arena.

15

The Move to Dressnitz

SARAH SOFER'S BLUE KERCHIEF WAS PULLED TIGHT. HER EYES CLOSED, she waved her hands three times over the *Shabbos* candles and stepped back. She sat at the *Shabbos* table and opened the *siddur* to the *Shabbos* services. She and Rabbi Sofer had good years together. Her brother had supported him three years beyond the original four years' stipend he had originally promised him. Her husband was a formidable scholar and teacher. True, they didn't have children. But Rabbi Sofer had so many students. Now, of course, there was another difficulty. But she would put on a brave face. And Rabbi Sofer need know nothing, as he had known nothing of it for a while.

Rabbi Sofer soon returned to his house, bringing the peace of *Shabbos* with him. Although he did not say *Shalom Aleichem*, he recited *Aishes Chayil*. "A woman of valor, who can find? . . . She girds herself with strength . . . all of her house is dressed in purple, she has made fine robes for herself, she is dressed in silk and crimson . . ."

Rabbi Sofer picked up the *Kiddush* cup and glanced at his wife. "Why are you wearing your weekday kerchief?"

On *Shabbos*, the women used to wear special kerchiefs embroidered with gold.

She put her closed hand to her mouth and gazed down at the table. Rabbi Sofer's eyes rested on her.

Tears sprang from her eyes and flowed onto her cheeks. "I—I don't have it . . . I didn't want to tell you . . . It isn't a matter for *Shabbos* . . ."

But Rabbi Sofer's patient silence drew her out. "Hirsch's business has not been going well. We kept it a secret. We didn't want to upset your learning. He has lost all of his money . . ."

Still, Rabbi Sofer remained silent.

"I had to pawn my *Shabbos* kerchief to pay for the *Kiddush* wine!"

"Don't cry, Sarah. Everything will be all right." He paced up and down the room. "I wish you had told me earlier. You should have told me. No! I cannot continue to be a burden on your brother. Do not worry. I will earn a living myself. Things will be all right."

The following week, Rabbi Sofer began considering what he could do to earn a living. Would he after all become a community rabbi? No. He would not reduce himself to using the Torah as a spade to dig with. And once he became the rabbi of the community, he would cease to be the master of his own time. Hadn't he earlier refused a match over this very point?

Then what would he do instead? He would learn a craft. Just as the sages of the Talmud earned their keep in simple professions, so would he work during the day and learn Torah in his spare time. He would become a tailor. People always needed tailors. He should be able to earn a modest living.

But he was already thirty years old. Could he now begin to learn a new craft?

In the meantime, as Rabbi Sofer considered his possibilities, he tried to maintain his learning schedule.

One day a poor person came in collecting charity. Rabbi Sofer had no more money to give him. "Wait a moment," Rabbi Sofer told the poor man.

He went into his other room and took a pair of scissors out of a drawer. His *tallis katan* was decorated with silver buttons. Rabbi Sofer took off his *tallis katan* and cut one of the buttons off. Putting the *tallis katan* back on, Rabbi Sofer went back to his room.

"Here," he told the poor man. "Take this button—it's made of silver—and sell it. Bring me back half of the money you get for it and keep the other half for yourself."

"Thank you, Rabbi Sofer. You are very generous."

Soon afterwards, another poor person came seeking a donation. Rabbi Sofer gave him another silver button.

One after another, the silver buttons disappeared. Soon there would be no silver left, no time left, no income left. He must come to a decision soon. Now the unthinkable began to intrude itself on his thoughts. Maybe, possibly, he would start exploring, inquiring if any community needed a rabbi. It was undignified—no, more than that, it was humiliating. Should a man have to go about selling his ability in Torah like a peddler hawking his tin pots? It was an insult to the Torah. And yet Rabbi Sofer and his wife must eat. The idea took on urgency.

But Rabbi Sofer was not forced to this extremity. Before he would have to stretch his hand out to others, others stretched their arms out to him.

The small community of Dressnitz invited Rabbi Sofer to become their rabbi. Rabbi Sofer considered that this was evidently the will of Heaven, and he consented to their offer.

According to government regulations, a Jewish community did not have the right to appoint a rabbi without the official consent of the Chief Rabbi of Moravia, who was at that time the well-known Torah scholar, Rabbi Mordechai Banet. Rabbi Sofer asked Rabbi Banet to invest him with official permission to head the community of Dressnitz and also to issue *halachic* decisions.

On the seventeenth of *Cheshvon*, 5554 (1793), Rabbi Mordechai Banet tendered him this document, which read, in part:

> *Yismach Moshe bematnas chelko*—Moshe, rejoice in the delight of Torah. This man's glorious light shines like a candelabra. This outstanding scholar, Moshe of Frankfurt, is to be *av beis din* of Dressnitz.
>
> He has learned deeply and he can deal with all problems. He is a master of the goodly merchandise of Torah.
>
> I have tested him and found that he is a master of Torah, knowing *Orech Chaim* and *Yoreh Deah* by heart, and with the ability to apply Torah reasoning as well.
>
> Now that he has attained this level, he shall be considered a rabbi who can lead a community and who can judge. I therefore crown him with the right to render legal decisions.
>
> May he grow ever greater in both heavenly and public affairs.
>
> Everyone is admonished to honor and love him, and not to contradict any of his words.
>
> May he who heeds these words merit to see the building of the Beis Hamikdash and the coming of the *Mashiach*.

In the meantime, Rabbi Sofer and his wife experienced more good fortune. A child joined their household. It was not, however, their own child that they brought up.

Although Rabbi Sofer felt that he could have asked Rabbi

Adler to pray to G-d on his behalf for children, he was afraid
that such prayers might, though efficacious, harm his wife if
she was naturally not able to give birth.

But a relative of Rabbi Sofer's wife had passed away and
left a small orphan girl homeless. Rabbi Sofer and his wife now
took this girl in. They would give her a home and bring her up.
And in turn, she would give them the feeling of bringing up
the child that they themselves could not have.

16

A Community Rabbi

"NO, PLEASE, I BEG YOU! LISTEN TO ME!"

Rabbi Sofer leaned out of the carriage at the crowd of Jews who stood in his way.

"Please, this is not right!"

But they would not listen to him. They quickly unharnessed the horses and led them away, as Rabbi Sofer watched helplessly.

Then six young men grabbed hold of the carriage shafts and began pulling the carriage themselves.

"No, please, this is not right!"

Rabbi Sofer could bear it no longer. What was this honor they were giving him? He did not want it. He did not need it. He swung open the carriage door and stepped to the ground.

"No, no!" the crowd protested.

A few of the older men immediately surrounded Rabbi

Sofer. "Please," one of them told him. "This is a matter of our joy. You must let us give you this honor."

Rabbi Sofer was silent a moment. Then he gave a nod of assent, and he climbed back into the carriage.

"Pull!" a voice cried out, and the carriage resumed turning its large, slow wheels into the town of Dressnitz.

Rabbi Sofer settled happily into his new home. He was paid a regular salary as rabbi, and he was free to learn and to teach as before. At first, the community did not have enough money to support a *yeshivah*, but over a period of time, Rabbi Sofer was able to persuade the community leaders to subsidize the learning of a number of students.

Rabbi Sofer had a large enough salary to support himself without worry and to maintain the *yeshivah*. For the rest of his life, he was never again to have a position that was so financially secure.

Rabbi Sofer was a dedicated and loving teacher. One day, a young person, aged sixteen or seventeen, walked into the *beis midrash*. He introduced himself to Rabbi Sofer as Pinchas Leib, and said that he very much wanted to learn Torah.

"Have you ever learned Torah until now?" asked Rabbi Sofer.

"No, not really." Pinchas gazed down at the floor.

Some of the other students, adolescents who had been learning since they had been toddlers, snickered. Was this ignoramus going to join their select group? They were the cream of the crop—they had memorized pages upon pages of Talmud and engaged in the most formidable theoretical discussions. They knew that they were brilliant and that they were the future leaders of Israel. It was truly a pleasant feeling to have. And now, this simple fellow, this bumpkin, was suggesting that he join them? It was something to laugh about. These few students looked expectantly at Rabbi Sofer, their eyes glinting merrily.

"Who is laughing here?" Rabbi Sofer spoke explosively, his intense eyes burning into his students until those who had snickered cringed under his gaze. "Shame on you! You do not have the right to judge who is fit to learn Torah and who is not fit to learn. You do not have the right to judge whom you shall allow into the *yeshivah* and whom you shall not. Perhaps they do so in other yeshivas—I don't know. But not here. Torah is the possession of all Jews. Whoever wants to learn is welcome to come and join us."

Rabbi Sofer accepted Pinchas Leib into the *yeshivah*, and he ordered the students to take turns learning with him every day.

Unfortunately, in addition to starting late, Pinchas Leib had a terrible memory. Even if he learned a *mishnah* a hundred times one day, by the next day he had forgotten it. Nevertheless, this young man had such a burning passion to learn Torah and he learned so diligently that over a period of time he became an outstanding student.

In the meantime, while Pinchas Leib was still quite young, Rabbi Sofer arranged a marriage between him and the orphan girl whom he had brought up.

Even after the couple was married, Rabbi Sofer gave them a dowry and supported them for several years at his table. Now Rabbi Sofer took care of both these young people as his own beloved children.

Soon after they were married, Rabbi Sofer had occasion to help another orphan.

Rabbi Sofer's second-floor apartment was directly over the home of Rabbi Nassan, the synagogue cantor. The windows of the house looked out over the cemetery. One evening, as Rabbi Sofer happened to glance out his window, he saw the spectral vision of Rabbi Nassan gliding through the dark and shadowy cemetery, dressed in shrouds.

The next morning, Rabbi Sofer told his students to say

102

Psalms on behalf of a man named Nassan. Rabbi Nassan himself was there and he too recited Psalms, not realizing that it was on his own behalf that he was doing so.

The next night, Rabbi Sofer looked out to see the same unearthly apparition wandering through the cemetery. Again, he told his students to pray for Rabbi Nassan.

That day, Rabbi Nassan fell ill.

On the third night, the same vision appeared to Rabbi Sofer. Soon afterwards, Rabbi Nassan passed away.

The wail of his baby child, Ezra, and the cry of his bereaved widow penetrated into Rabbi Sofer's apartment.

Rabbi Sofer considered: Why had he been vouchsafed this vision of Rabbi Nassan's impending death? He decided that he had a responsibility to take care of the orphaned child. Rabbi Sofer had the child brought up in his own house. He paid the boy's mother to nurse him and the boy's sister to watch over him. Whenever Ezra cried, Rabbi Sofer would knock on the floor until the boy's mother came upstairs to take care of him.

In addition, Rabbi Sofer raised another orphan: his sister's son, Shmuel Strauss.

Rabbi Sofer now began his career in rendering *halachic* decisions. Rabbi Sofer's style was direct and firm. Once he made a decision, he did not vacillate, but took full responsibility for his stance.

In earlier letters, beginning in 1787, he had discussed *halachah* without rendering *halachic* decisions. The first known letter that Rabbi Sofer wrote that gave a *halachic* decision was written in 5556 (1796). Rabbi Sofer was turned to by Jews in his geographical region, with whom he shared a common history and background of customs, including Torah scholars in towns such as Semnitz and Boskowitz.

Rabbi Sofer began to gain a reputation as a leading Torah authority. His letters ultimately comprised the material of his magnum opus, which he titled Chasam Sofer, over 1200 *halachic* responses dealing with a wide range of *halachic* issues. And it is as the Chasam Sofer that he is referred to by tens of thousands of disciples and their disciples and all students of Torah to the present day.

It was also in Dressnitz that Rabbi Sofer wrote most of his poetry, which has been collected and published as *Shiras Moshe*, "The Song of Moshe." Rabbi Sofer composed most of his poetry between *Yom Kippur* and *Sukkos*. Rabbi Sofer wrote poetry on the occasion of the holidays and of *Shabbos*. He also had the custom of writing a poem at the beginning of every notebook of Torah thoughts that he began. He would treat in verse form an ethical theme related to the topic that he was dealing with.

Rabbi Sofer also began to get involved in public concerns. It was his role to deliver talks in the synagogue. In these talks, he dealt with many of the social issues of the day. Rabbi Sofer's talks were firmly embedded in the traditional teachings of the Torah in its four aspects of *p'shat*-simple meaning, *derash*-homiletics, *remez*-hints and *sod*-mysticism. He was a very eloquent speaker who appeared to speak easily and well. But at the same time, when he spoke, Rabbi Sofer was imbued with the fear of Heaven. In later years, Rabbi Sofer once told his son, Rabbi Avraham Shmuel, "Believe me, when I stand before the *aron kodesh* to speak, if someone were to cut me, not a drop of blood would come out."

In those times, the government had begun drafting Jewish young men into the army. Because draftees were often those who came from the lowest rungs of society, some Jews expressed their approval of the draft. It served, they argued, to remove negative elements from Jewish society. But Rabbi Sofer disagreed with this heartless attitude toward one's fellow Jews and he rebuked those who held this callous opinion.

Rabbi Sofer also addressed other communal problems.

There was insufficient financial support for poor children and Torah students; taxes were imposed unfairly so that the poor paid an inordinate share; at times, leaders of the community and the *chevrah kaddisha* took advantage of the poor and of strangers; some people had become lax in their *Shabbos* observance; others attended theaters; still others played cards. Thus Rabbi Sofer had to deal both with age-old problems of corruption and the particular problem of his day, Jews beginning to imitate gentile fashion and slipping away from their commitment to Torah.

Soon after Rabbi Sofer came to Dressnitz, his brother-in-law began to gradually recover his former economic status. It was clear that Hirsch Yerwitz's loss of income had been brought about from Heaven so that Rabbi Sofer would be forced to accept the role of chief rabbi and thus spread the light of Torah to others.

Nevertheless, Rabbi Sofer did not grow entirely reconciled to this. In subsequent years, he wrote to a student, "Regarding accepting a community position and receiving community money, this is very difficult. But I am myself in such an unenviable position of receiving public funds, for my many sins."

Several years later, Hirsch Yerwitz passed away, and his widow remarried. When the widow subsequently died, she left her substantial fortune to Rabbi Sofer. Most of the money that he had came from this inheritance.

Now that Rabbi Sofer was becoming famous, various communities in the area of Moravia and Western Hungary began vying to have him move to their communities.

In 5558 (1798), after having served as rabbi of Dressnitz for four years, Rabbi Sofer received an offer to be appointed *av beis din* of Mattersdorf, Hungary. Mattersdorf was one of the towns known as the "Seven Communities," which were owned by the Eszterhazy magnates. It was also a major Jewish

105

community. Any rabbi who received such a post was automatically a man to be reckoned with.

Rabbi Sofer accepted the position. Immediately afterwards, however, Prossnitz offered him the identical position. Rabbi Sofer had lived in Prossnitz earlier, and he would have preferred to serve there. And there were those who, faced with such a dilemma, would have reneged on their earlier acceptance. But, as in the case of his engagement contract, Rabbi Sofer was scrupulously honest. He wrote back to the community of Prossnitz, "I will give thanks to G-d for your offer. But I have already accepted the post in Mattersdorf, and I cannot present them with excuses about why I have changed my mind, which is the custom. If I disappoint them, they will say that I am untrustworthy, and this will cause a desecration of G-d's name."

17

Chief Rabbi of Mattesdorf

"WHY ARE YOU INQUIRING SO MUCH ABOUT THE AUTHORIZATION TO receive this *get*? Is there a problem?" Rabbi Sofer asked.

Rabbi Meshullam Igra (Tismenitzer) looked at him quizzically.

"I mean, the only reason to check a *harshaah* (power of attorney) so carefully is because the Rivash says that one must make sure that the people who made it were credible. But the rabbis who signed this *harshaah* are trustworthy."

"Times are changing, Rabbi Sofer. Surely you know that."

"But these rabbis—"

"It is not the rabbis. Today we have to be concerned with the messengers."

"Do we have to take it so far?"

"So far? Look about you, Rabbi Sofer. See how far the pilings are slipping. See how the moorings are crumbling."

On his way to Mattersdorf, in a coach led by a high-spirited, white horse and a rough, laughing coachman, Rabbi Sofer had stopped over in the city of Pressburg.

Here, he had called upon Rabbi Meshullam Igra of Tismenitz, the *av beis din* and an exceedingly brilliant scholar.

When Rabbi Sofer took leave of Rabbi Tismenitzer, Rabbi Tismenitzer accompanied him downstairs and to the courtyard gate.

The men in the *beis midrash* stood up and watched in silent astonishment as the aged sage accompanied the tall, young rabbi.

One of the men stood at the *beis midrash* door and unobtrusively watched Rabbi Tismenitzer give a blessing to Rabbi Sofer at the courtyard gate. Rabbi Sofer bowed his head and walked away, and the bowed-over Rabbi Tismenitzer walked back across the courtyard to the *beis midrash*.

"Rabbi Tismenitzer—" the man dogged Rabbi Tismenitzer's footsteps.

Rabbi Tismenitzer turned. "Yes?"

"If you don't mind—if I may ask—why have you shown this young man so much honor? You do not honor rabbis who have the most important posts in this way."

"Yes, you are right. But look well on Rabbi Sofer. He is a great *tzaddik* and Torah scholar." Rabbi Tismenitzer took a few more steps. He stopped and turned back to the man. "He is going to Mattersdorf now. But his Torah will flow out of Pressburg." And Rabbi Tismenitzer continued in his praise.

From Pressburg, Rabbi Sofer continued to Vienna. When he arrived there on a Wednesday, he realized that if he continued according to schedule, he would have to *daven Shacharis* on Thursday morning without a *minyan*, and miss the Torah reading.

Rabbi Sofer decided that he would therefore leave Vienna early, travelling throughout the night.

With the rising of the sun, Rabbi Sofer's carriage entered Mattersdorf. Men whispered to one another as Rabbi Sofer entered the synagogue for *Shacharis*. "It is Rabbi Sofer!"

"But he was supposed to arrive here later today. We had a whole welcoming ceremony planned!"

"It's a good sign. It shows he isn't interested in ceremonies, but in teaching Torah."

Rabbi Sofer was surrounded by several students who had accompanied him from Dressnitz. One of these students was the slow learner, Pinchas Leib. He applied himself with such diligence that he eventually became a judge in Mattersdorf and afterwards rabbi of Neuzatch.

Although Rabbi Sofer was made several tempting offers to move to other communities during the years he served as rabbi of Mattersdorf, he remained there for nine years.

For these years, Rabbi Sofer continued the custom he had begun in Dressnitz of learning only standing up. In addition, he never went to bed. He would learn in his room, standing at a window. Whenever he grew sleepy, he would stand in a basin of cold water. If he felt that he could no longer avoid sleep, he would place a key under his forehead. When the key would fall, the noise would wake him and he would resume his learning. Thus, for fourteen years, Rabbi Sofer only took short naps.

In the first year of Rabbi Sofer's stay in Mattersdorf, he was visited by Rabbi David Deutsch, the Rabbi of Neustadt, an outstanding student of Rabbi Yechezkel Landau, the *Noda Biyehudah*. (Of all the published responsa in the *Noda Biyehudah*, nearly forty are addressed to him!) Although Rabbi Deutsch was much older than Rabbi Sofer, he insisted on referring to Rabbi Sofer respectfully as "Rabbi."

"Bless me, Rabbi," requested Rabbi Deutsch one day as he took leave of Rabbi Sofer.

"Who am I to do such a thing?" Rabbi Sofer replied. "To the

109

contrary, I would like you to bless me!"

"Please, I ask you," Rabbi Deutsch insisted, and Rabbi Sofer blessed him.

"And now I must ask you to bless me," Rabbi Sofer asked in his turn.

But in his humility, Rabbi Deutsch could not bring himself to do so.

Later, Rabbi Deutsch told those around him, "Rabbi Sofer's face is the face of Yeshayahu the Prophet."

In Mattersdorf, Rabbi Sofer was often ill. Once, he wrote to Rabbi Deutsch, "Unfortunately, for the last seven weeks, I have been house-ridden with a cough. A number of times, I was in great danger. But thank G-d, I have arrived at this point. At any rate, my work—that is to say, the work of teaching Torah—is being done by others. The doctors have forbidden me to do any teaching myself. I tell the lesson to one of my students, and he repeats it to the others in my presence. May G-d have mercy and send me a complete recovery speedily."

This student whom Rabbi Sofer referred to was Rabbi Meir Asch (actually an abbreviation of Eisenstadt, his real family name), who later wrote the scholarly work *Imrei Aish*. Rabbi Sofer thought very highly of him and said that in twenty years he had not seen any other Torah scholar as familiar with the texts. Rabbi Meir Asch later married the daughter of Rabbi David Deutsch.

Rabbi Sofer engaged intensively in study of *Kabbalah*. To this purpose, he possessed many texts, both printed and hand-written manuscripts. He purchased many of these from Rabbi Shmuel Chaim, *av beis din* of Frankfurt, in whose margins Rabbi Shmuel Chaim had often added his own comments.

Rabbi Sofer used to say, in opposition to those who disparaged the learning of *Kabbalah*, "Whoever openly denigrates the hidden Torah secretly denigrates the revealed

Torah." But, like his two teachers, Rabbi Adler and Rabbi Horowitz, Rabbi Sofer never mentioned the teachings of the *Zohar* in any of his talks.

Rabbi Sofer urged Rabbi Meir Asch to learn *Kabbalah* and offered to teach him. But Rabbi Meir Asch refused. "*Kabbalah* is not for the likes of men like me," he argued. But in later years, he expressed his regret at having had such an attitude.

And so Rabbi Sofer applied himself to his intensive studies and work of teaching. But he was finding things very difficult. Although Mattersdorf was an important community, it did not have enough money to pay Rabbi Sofer adequately. More than that, the community was not able to properly maintain the *yeshivah*. And finally, there were many familial disputes in Mattersdorf, and this squabbling was not to his liking. So when an offer came from Dressnitz in 1801, inviting him to return, Rabbi Sofer seriously considered the proposal, until the leaders of Mattersdorf increased his salary.

Rabbi Sofer found himself as a community rabbi in the midst of vexing issues that swirled about the religious community. In 1801, he was asked whether a follower of Shabbesai Tzvi should be excommunicated if the possibility existed of his converting to Christianity. Rabbi Sofer replied that under any circumstances, such a person should be excommunicated, unless such an act would cause him to baptize his children. However, there is no evidence that there were any *Shabbatian* Jews in Mattersdorf itself. On an issue dealing with societal mores, Rabbi Sofer was more yielding. Although he had condemned card playing while in Dressnitz, he now compromised and allowed the playing of cards during gentile holidays.

One evening, as Rabbi Sofer slept, he had a vision of five Torah scrolls wrapped in black mantles.

"Why are you in black?" Rabbi Sofer asked.

"Don't you know the custom of the city of your birth,

111

Frankfurt-am-Main?" the scrolls replied. "Don't you recall that on a public fast day, the Torah scrolls are wrapped in black?"

Rabbi Sofer awoke, and he had the darkest forebodings about what this dream had come to tell him.

Soon a letter arrived in Mattersdorf bearing the tragic news: at the age of fifty-eight, Rabbi Nassan Adler had passed away.

"Now I understand the meaning of this dream," Rabbi Sofer wrote. "The Torah mourns over the death of the *tzaddik*, my teacher. Who will fix the rift? Who will stand in the breach? I saw Rabbi Adler sitting and teaching like Moshe himself from the mouth of G-d. I ran after him hundreds of miles. I abandoned the house of my mother and the home of my birth, as everyone knows, and I and my father did his will though it caused us suffering.

"And now," Rabbi Sofer grieved, "I did not merit to see Rabbi Adler when he passed away. I did not merit to let my tears drop on the grave of the man of G-d. I did not merit to see his face right before he passed away."

This truly left Rabbi Sofer feeling bereft. If he had been present at Rabbi Adler's death, Rabbi Sofer wrote, "his soul would have come upon me, as did Eliyahu's soul upon Elisha."

The same day that the news arrived, Rabbi Sofer delivered a eulogy in the synagogue, sitting on the floor in mourning.

But although the old world was quickly disappearing and leaving Rabbi Sofer more and more alone as a leader in the European Jewish community, his powers now increased, as though Rabbi Adler's spirit had rested upon him.

Rabbi Sofer himself reported that "I learned from my pious teacher, Rabbi Nassan Adler, that as long as the teacher is alive, his student cannot attain his full stature. We see this in the case of Yehoshua, the student of Moshe, who was not leader until Moshe passed away. Similarly, we do not learn about G-d's presence resting on Yitzchak until after Avraham died. Also, as long as Yaakov was in his father's house, G-d did not speak to him. But as soon as he left, G-d came to him in a vision."

Now, as the pillars of Rabbi Sofer's upbringing dissolved into insubstantiality, Rabbi Sofer was embodying their powers and bringing them to bear upon all that he touched.

But in this world, even spirit must rest upon pillars of the physical. Again, Rabbi Sofer found that his stipend was not enough to support him, and again the community was not able to support the *yeshivah* to his satisfaction.

In 5562 (1802), Rabbi Adler accepted the petition of the town of Neustadt (today Nove Mesto in Slovakia) to become its *av beis din*.

"Why are you leaving us?" one of the members of Mattersdorf asked Rabbi Adler. "Why are you so dissatisfied?"

"You are too quick to judge me," replied Rabbi Sofer. "It is true: some rabbis are like oxen. If an ox is grazing at the foot of a hill, he will still run up to the top of the hill to find yet more to eat. There are some rabbis who, no matter how well-off they are, still run from city to city and from post to post trying to get a better position. But as for me, I am not like that. I would like to stay. But what can I do, when I cannot even make ends meet?"

Meanwhile, Rabbi Sofer sent the community of Neustadt a list of conditions that they would be required to meet before he would accept the post. The people of Neustadt accepted these conditions. Yet, Rabbi Sofer still delayed. Tempers frayed; people became anxious; what was keeping Rabbi Sofer from answering them now? But they still had no reply.

18

Fire and Ruin

THE SYNAGOGUE WAS PACKED. RABBI SOFER STOOD BEFORE THE *aron kodesh* and gave his last sermon in Mattersdorf. Next *Shabbos*, he would be in Neustadt. The people strained to hear his every word. It was the last chance that they would have.

Soon after the talk, there was a smell of something burning. There was a wisp of smoke, a hint of a flame, a harried woman running down the street holding a baby, crying out, "Fire, fire!" People looked up the road from which the woman had run: smoke was pouring out of the whiskey distillery, thick and gray billows, as huge, orange flames danced up behind the windows like great, glowing sheets.

"The distillery! The infamous distillery!" That was the distillery that was open on *Shabbos*. People remembered that when Rabbi Yirmiyah had left his position as rabbi of

Mattersdorf to become *av beis din* in Santov, he had threatened the Jew who was renting it, "Because you keep this distillery open on *Shabbos*, it will burn down on *Shabbos*!" The man had grimaced angrily and contemptuously turned his face away. Now Rabbi Yirmiyah's words were proving prophetic.

The flames leaped from the distillery and leaped onto the roof of the adjacent building. The adjoining roof quickly blazed into flame. From roof to roof and house to house, the terrible conflagration spread.

By the time *Shabbos* was over, most of the Jewish quarter was in charred ruins.

"I am not leaving you now," said Rabbi Sofer to the delegation of Jews who came to him in mourning. "I will not desert you." Rabbi Sofer was the leader of Mattersdorf. He would not abandon the people in their trouble.

The next morning, Rabbi Sofer surveyed the terrible destruction that the fire had wrought. Houses had been reduced to charred, smoking ruins. Entire families, small children, invalids and old people had been left homeless, all their possessions burned.

In the whirlwind of events and emergency planning, Rabbi Sofer did not have the time to reply to Neustadt. Only afterwards did he write back and decline their offer, on the grounds that the emergency conditions in Mattersdorf demanded that he remain there.

Rabbi Sofer took charge of the efforts to help the people who had suffered in the terrible fire. In response to his requests, donations poured in from many other Jewish communities. Temporary wooden buildings were set up to house those Jews who had been left homeless.

One evening, Rabbi Sofer had a dream that a scribe had made *tefillin* but had left out the ridges on the *batim*—the outer leather box. Rabbi Sofer was accustomed to having meaningful dreams and visions, and when he awoke, he pondered what this dream could mean. The following two nights, the dream recurred.

Finally, Rabbi Sofer realized what the dream was telling him. He was the scribe—the *sofer*. The Hebrew word for box is the same as the word for house. He had left the temporary housing where the Jews were living without partitions—the *charitzin*. Because of the emergency conditions, many families were living together within one large room, and this did not provide modest living conditions. Rabbi Sofer immediately ordered that partitions be erected to separate the different families.

Rabbi Sofer found that his efforts to rebuild the original, permanent houses were meeting with a great deal of contention. The law stated that only a person who owned an apartment or land had the right to settle in the "Seven Communities" of which Mattersdorf was one. In order for Jews to be able to live in Mattersdorf, each Jew owned part of a house. One Jew owned a top floor, another a bottom floor; one Jew owned the inside of a house and the other the back of a house.

Now, when the houses were being rebuilt, arguments broke out regarding what the original boundaries had been. Often, two or more Jews claimed the same piece of house and the land that it stood on. Rabbi Sofer spent a great deal of effort resolving these disputes justly.

Out of the smoking wreckage, new houses were going up. But some people thought only of themselves.

One insolent man went to the city judges and complained that Rabbi Sofer was arbitrarily dividing property, taking what belonged to one person and giving it to another.

The judges came to Rabbi Sofer and asked him the basis of his decisions and how he knew the way to divide the houses.

Rabbi Sofer took an ax in his hand and brought the judges

through the crowded street to the wall of a burned house that still stood. "Look here." Rabbi Sofer swung the ax and cracked open the end of the wall. "You can see that there are two sets of bricks below the plaster facing in different directions. So this has to be the dividing line between two properties."

"That's extraordinary," one of the judges replied. "How did you know to break open the plaster right here?"

Rabbi Sofer pointed up toward the top of the wall. "You can see up there where the plaster is discolored by a leak. That clearly shows that the wall was poorly joined at that point, which allowed the leak to form."

The judges were astonished at Rabbi Sofer's expertise in the practical aspect of these matters, and they put their complete confidence in him.

In another case, the community and a widow entered into a dispute over payment for damages. The widow's house had adjoined the synagogue. When the fire had spread close to her house, members of the community had torn down her roof to prevent the fire from crossing over it to the synagogue. As a result, both the synagogue and the widow's house had been saved. Now the woman demanded that the community pay for her roof. The community refused. "If we hadn't pulled it off," one of the men claimed, "the fire would have burned it down. We don't owe you anything."

The dispute came before Rabbi Sofer, and he ruled that according to the strict letter of the law the community was right. However, when one took into consideration the particular and tragic circumstances of the case, one had to temper justice with mercy. In consequence, Rabbi Sofer ruled in the woman's favor.

As a result of this fire, Rabbi Sofer himself suffered great poverty. He was forced to record his monetary notes in the notebooks usually dedicated to his Torah insights.

But despite his poverty and troubles, Rabbi Sofer gave

himself over to helping others. Not only did he help those in his community, but he even made the time to respond to *halachic* questions that people sent him by mail. He was proving that he could be a Torah leader under the most trying circumstances.

In this same year that Rabbi Sofer committed himself to remaining with the community of Mattersdorf, news came that Rabbi Meshullam Tismenitzer, *av beis din* of Pressburg, had passed away. He had predicted to those around him that Rabbi Sofer's Torah would flow out of Pressburg. But there seemed to be no sign of that now.

In 5562 (1803), another community—Yarmuth—offered Rabbi Sofer a position. Rabbi Sofer refused. He was dedicated to his present obligations.

Then, in 5565 (1805), another of the great pillars of his youth that had supported Rabbi Sofer crumbled away. On the fourth of *Tammuz*, Rabbi Pinchas Horowitz died at the age of seventy-five. He had served as rabbi of Frankfurt-am-Main for thirty-three years. In that time, he had taught thousands of students, but his most famous student had been Rabbi Moshe Sofer.

19

To Pressburg

THE CITY OF PRESSBURG (PRESENTLY KNOWN AS BRATISLAVA, Czechoslovakia) had been without a chief rabbi for five years. Because of the new spirit of modernism and the lack of leadership, this city, which had been a center of piety, was in danger of becoming a worldly Jewish community with deteriorating levels of observance.

The officers of the Pressburg community met to appoint a new chief rabbi. Three candidates were chosen: Rabbi Akiva Eiger, then rabbi of Markisch-Friedland; Rabbi Boruch Frenkel, rabbi of Leipnik, and Rabbi Shalom Ullman, the rabbi of Lakenbach, who was then rabbi in Fraunkirchen.

In the middle of the long, circular discussion, one of the delegates declared, "Gentleman! I wish to propose a man whose name we have not mentioned before, a man whose name has been praised and told through many communities, a great rabbi whom you can accept with a full heart and who, furthermore, is of our own communities.

"Gentlemen, this is a man filled with fiery adherence to Torah, a natural ruler whose schooling was deep and whose dedication is total.

"Gentlemen, this man's goodness is as the lily of the valley—as the turtledove bred for felicity and the cedar tree for might; as the bright pomegranate is filled with good, as the green wood is rich with sap, as the tapped well brings forth sweet water.

"Gentlemen, let us brush aside the clouds of doubt and choose the man who is close to our hearts and close to our customs and proximity.

"Gentlemen, let us choose Rabbi Moshe Sofer, Rav of Mattersdorf. We have all heard of his great wisdom in Torah, his holiness, his pristine character. He is certainly fit and more than fit to give this position honor even as it may honor him. Why should we not choose him, someone who is so near to us, rather than another rabbi, although great and worthy, from afar?"

"Indeed, I now recall," called out another delegate. "Rabbi Meshullam Tismenitzer had predicted in his holy words that Rabbi Moshe Sofer would come to Pressburg, and that his Torah would shine to the Jews here in exile. Let us choose him, for it was the inspired wish of a tzaddik. The fire of his Torah will inflame our hearts. Let us name him and peaceably depart."

"No! We cannot!" another man spoke, his black, vast coat wrapped about. "It would be underhanded not to stick to the names that we had announced. We will be considered devious and it will be said that what occurred here can be overruled. We must be limited by our original decision and choose from these three names or be subject to derision. Come, no ruses, and we will not be blamed; let us be done with it, the people shall praise us; and we shall have no reason to fear critics."

Thus did the discussion circumambulate, turn and percolate, until one perspicacious man spoke and gained the favor of the company. "I propose," he said, "that we put the matter to a vote of chance and choose lots. In this way, we shall accrue no blame, and not be accused of impropriety. Rather, we shall give this matter over without fear to the One Who rules the earth, the ocean and the sky. He shall choose and make the motion."

The proposition was considered and thought good, and the delegation performed its duty and chose a wooden bowl from which to draw the lots.

"The post has gone to Rabbi Moshe Sofer!" exclaimed the man who chose the paper from the bowl. The company accepted his decree in equanimity, and each man turned to his home, prepared to share the news to cheer Rabbi Sofer's soul.

Soon a letter was written, signed, sealed and placed within the post carriage; the horses galloped, stirred up dust on the trammeled road, skirted the villages along the long route until the postman came to Mattersdorf and sought out Rabbi Sofer. He tendered him the sealed letter, contents concealed until the moment that Rabbi Sofer should gaze upon their honeyed words.

Rabbi Sofer broke the seal, read the calligraphic text, considered and nodded his head, considered more and made his decision. Rabbi Sofer returned to his learning in his room, and no more than faint murmurs could be heard.

The news spread throughout Mattersdorf: Rabbi Sofer was planning to leave them! Rabbi Sofer, their leader, was stepping down and leaving his post. He had led them; he had rebuilt them, nurtured them, brought them back to life after the terrible fire had almost destroyed Mattersdorf.

A murmur of voices, a clattering of wooden heels, a throng

of men, women and children, rabbis and laymen, scholars and craftsmen, approached Rabbi Sofer's residence. Rabbi Sofer glanced up from his window.

"Stay, Rabbi Sofer! Do not leave us!" pleaded the people, standing before his window as he gazed down at them with warm eyes. One of the rabbis stepped forward and beseeched Rabbi Sofer to reconsider. "Are we not a community as well? Do we not need sustenance and assistance as well? Do not therefore turn to those who ask for you in foreign parts, as a father who does not abandon his child to raise an orphan."

Rabbi Sofer stepped to the window. "I have considered your words, good people. I shall take them into account. Please do not be sad of heart. All that G-d does is for the best. Wait for *Shabbos*, and then I shall give you my decision." Rabbi Sofer retreated from the window and sat down at his desk. Taking pen to paper, he wrote a series of paragraphs in his elegant handwriting. Folding the letter and sealing it, Rabbi Sofer called for the *shammes* and instructed him to deliver the letter to one of the heads of the community.

Shabbos morning came. The synagogue was packed. The people were squeezed together, the men wrapped in their *talleisim* rubbing shoulders and upstairs, the women pressed together on the benches, leaning forward toward the balcony.

Rabbi Sofer stepped up before the *aron kodesh*. "My friends," he announced, "I have made my decision. I am going to leave Mattersdorf and go to Pressburg."

A murmur of disappointment raced through the synagogue.

He continued speaking. "I have weighed the matter carefully and made sure that I fulfilled all my obligations. This week, I sent a letter to one of the community leaders. In that letter, I mentioned a few reasonable conditions that I said would have to be met if I were to remain here. I have not received a reply to my letter. I must therefore assume that you have decided that it is acceptable to you that I go to Pressburg."

Pandemonium broke out in the synagogue. A number of leaders of the community stood up and cried out, "We were never informed about this letter. Who was responsible for this?"

"Rabbi Avraham! Rabbi Avraham!" the voice of the crowd exclaimed. Word ran through the people like electricity. It was Rabbi Avraham who had withheld the letter and caused Rabbi Sofer to leave. He was the one who had betrayed them!

The people streamed to Rabbi Avraham, pushing against him. "What did you do? Why did you hide the letter?"

Rabbi Avraham raised his wrinkled hands in supplication. "Please, good people, please. You are quite mistaken. I have no knowledge of this matter. The person whom you are seeking is Rabbi Mordechai."

"Rabbi Mordechai! Rabbi Mordechai!" The mob left Rabbi Avraham and turned to Rabbi Mordechai.

Rabbi Mordechai stood in his place, unmoving and calm, facing the crowd with tight lips. He was surrounded by red, angry faces. Some men even waved their fists in the air. "Punish him! He has driven Rabbi Sofer away!"

"Quiet! Quiet, people," shouted out one of the community leaders. "Silence! Right now!" With difficulty, some of the men succeeded in silencing the excited crowd.

"Now tell us," called out one man, "did you withhold Rabbi Sofer's letter from us for yourself?"

Rabbi Mordechai wet his lips with his tongue. "Hear me, good people," he said in a firm, loud voice. "It is true that, as Rabbi Sofer has just told you, he sent me a list of his conditions for staying in Mattersdorf, and that he made me responsible to bring this letter to Rabbi Avraham."

There was another angry uproar from the people again.

"Everyone knows that I am a willing servant to do anything that Rabbi Sofer asks for," Rabbi Mordechai continued. "But now I had to take counsel with myself. I want to see the best for myself and for all the people of Mattersdorf. But there is one value that I hold dear over all others. That value is truth. And what is the truth in this case? That no matter how much we love Rabbi Sofer, we must admit that it is best for all the people of Israel that we allow him to go where he wants to go, to Pressburg. We cannot confine him here.

"Pressburg is a great city, and G-d has given our rabbi the opportunity to go there and do great things for the sake of Torah. We have to face it squarely—Mattersdorf is too small a town for a man of Rabbi Sofer's stature. He must go to Pressburg, where he will be able to grow to his full eminence and enlighten all the communities of the exile.

"Will we, in our desire to keep Rabbi Sofer for ourselves, prevent him from reaching the heights that he is able to attain? Will we prevent him from becoming not only an outstanding rabbi for one town but a leading rabbi for the entire generation?"

The synagogue was silent.

"Gentlemen, I ask you," Rabbi Mordechai said. "Which of you would take responsibility for such a decision?

"And so because I had the best interests of Rabbi Sofer and all Jews at heart, I secreted that letter and did not share it with anyone else. Gentlemen, now decide if I acted foolishly or wisely."

The people were subdued. There were a few angry outbursts, but the mood had changed around. The people realized that they could no longer change the fate of a generation.

The more level-headed in the community realized that Rabbi Sofer really wished to leave Mattersdorf. If he had desired to remain, he would have reconsidered the matter immediately upon learning that his message had not been delivered. These people realized that they no more had the right to hold on to Rabbi Sofer than did an infant to hold on to its mother when she had to leave it for some time.

Surrounded by a circle of students and colleagues, Rabbi Sofer walked sedately home. The die had been cast. He was going to Pressburg.

20

Introduction to Pressburg

"DO NOT COME TO PRESSBURG! MOST OF THE TORAH SCHOLARS OF our community, including the most outstanding leaders, oppose your moving into our community. Remain in Mattersdorf, where your abilities will be appreciated."

Rabbi Sofer sat in a hostelry in a little town on the way to Pressburg and read this letter with bewilderment. Was this true? Should he go back to Mattersdorf? Or was the letter no more than the malicious act of some scheming individual? In the midst of Rabbi Sofer's deliberations, he said to himself, "In the past, whenever I have had a difficult problem, Rabbi Mordechai Brode has come and helped me. But this time, I am on my own."

There was a sudden rattle of hooves, horses neighing, the voice of a coachman. A moment later, Rabbi Brode stepped into the inn.

"My dear friend," Rabbi Brode said, striding forward to Rabbi Sofer, "I am familiar with the matter that is troubling you. Do not be afraid. G-d is with you. He will cast down your enemies, and you will succeed in all that you do."

Rabbi Sofer bowed his head down in silent gratitude to this miraculous man, learned in the mysteries of *Kabbalah*, who had so fortuitously come to him with this reassuring message. "Thank you for these encouraging words, Rabbi Brode."

Rabbi Sofer looked up. He was staggered. Rabbi Brode was not before him! He had disappeared into the very air! Rabbi Sofer took a hold of himself. He realized that he had been shown from Heaven that he should continue on his way to Pressburg.

As he continued travelling, Rabbi Sofer sent ahead an open letter in which he announced what section of the Talmud he would be discussing in his first talk to the community, as was the custom.

With a thin wind stinging his cheeks, Rabbi Sofer entered the city of Pressburg, met by the city leaders and a crowd of well-wishers. They huddled against the swift breeze and turned to enter the city and bring Rabbi Sofer and his entourage to his new home.

The days passed smoothly. Rabbi Sofer adjusted himself quietly to Pressburg and prepared for his new duties. *Shabbos* was drawing closer, his first *Shabbos* as rabbi of Pressburg. Friday morning came. Swiftly the afternoon overtook the day, and then the afternoon flew on white wings of cloud into the sapphire embrace of *Shabbos*.

Late that night, as Rabbi Sofer leaned over a volume of Torah, an image appeared at the window. Moments later, someone knocked at the door, and an old friend of Rabbi Sofer's entered.

"Rabbi Sofer, I will be brief," said the short man. "The boy who serves you . . . has been bought over!"

"Meaning?"

"He has been bribed to copy out your Torah thoughts from your notebooks on the Talmud passage that you plan to speak on tomorrow in your *drashah*."

"They have corrupted my own servant?"

"Yes, Rabbi Sofer. You must know that not everyone was pleased with your coming here. In particular, there is one wealthy family who had hoped that one of their own, a man named Rabbi Zalman Leib, would become the new Chief Rabbi. They are the ones who sent you that letter to return to Mattersdorf, and now they are the ones who have engineered this. These people have spent the last several days studying your notes. When you stand up to give your talk, they will refute you on every point. Their intent is to confuse you and to make you appear unlearned. Then they will have a chance to call for you to be fired and for Rabbi Zalman Leib to take your place."

Rabbi Sofer walked over to the bookshelf and pulled out the first volume of *Gemara* that came to his hand. He opened the volume, which happened to be *Sanhedrin*, at random. Pointing to a few lines on the page, he said, "Tomorrow, with G-d's help, instead of the talk that I had planned, I will give a talk on this topic."

Evening blossomed into morning. *Shacharis* passed and then *Mussaf*.

Rabbi Sofer stood up to deliver his talk. To the astonishment and bewilderment of his antagonists, his sermon was a brilliant examination of the passage in *Sanhedrin*. Rabbi Sofer's adversaries were left speechless before both his ruse and genius.

Rabbi Sofer was not finished, however. He proceeded to give an extensive talk on *Aggadah*, based on the week's *parshah* of *Lech Lechah*. In the midst of his talk, Rabbi Sofer commented, "It is possible that some of the members of this community were eager to appoint me as chief rabbi because I am childless. You may have thought that it will cost you little to support me. You may have thought that without family, my influence will be limited. But if this was anyone's intention, allow me to disabuse him of the notion. In Mattersdorf, I did not have children—true. But here, I will have children. With the help of G-d and to the best of my ability, I will build good buildings, and I will make the influence of Torah felt."

With these challenging words, Rabbi Sofer stepped down and returned to his seat.

The coming week, the Torah scholars of Pressburg visited Rabbi Sofer and entered into conversation with him, bringing him their questions in *halachah* and *Aggadah*. Among them was Rabbi Zalman Leib himself.

When Rabbi Zalman Leib heard Rabbi Sofer's discussions of Torah, he realized how great Rabbi Sofer was. He was transformed from an opponent of Rabbi Sofer to being his warm-hearted supporter. The two men drew close to one another and eventually Rabbi Sofer helped Rabbi Zalman Leib become rabbi of Serdahely.

When Rabbi Sofer first came to Pressburg, the city had slipped from total loyalty to tradition and was somewhat influenced by the tides of reform and assimilation. Like other cities such as Prague and Nikolsburg, Pressburg was being influenced by new times. Some businessmen from Pressburg, for instance, wrote to Rabbi Sofer asking him to grant them permission to engage in certain acts so that they would not appear strange in the eyes of the gentiles with whom they had to deal. They informed Rabbi Sofer that they dressed in gentile garb and that they cut their hair and trimmed their beards both on *Chol Hamoed* and during the days of *sefiras ha-omer*. In addition, their wives and daughters went so far as to adorn themselves with eye makeup and to wear wigs rather than kerchiefs.

With Rabbi Sofer's arrival, this tendency was gradually halted and eventually reversed. This monumental achievement was attained by the application by Rabbi Sofer of all the different aspects that made him outstanding: his greatness in learning, his moral authority, his energy and application, his certainty in the rightness of his cause, and his decisive communal measures, which strengthened and institutionalized the office of the Orthodox rabbinate so that after his death his influence did not wane.

In the same year of Rabbi Sofer's installation as rabbi of Pressburg, the issue of Jewish political reform *vis-a-vis* the gentile government was a volatile topic. The Jews of Hungary petitioned the Parliament, known as the *Sejm*, to be given rights equal to those of the non-noble gentile classes. They asked that this not be granted at the price of losing their communal autonomy as Jewish communities. In addition, they requested that Jews be allowed to earn a livelihood as farmers, manufacturers, artisans, merchants and hawkers. Until this time, Jews were only allowed to earn work as merchants, and for many Jews, this meant great poverty.

The government's immediate response was to grant the Jews a right of a very different sort: the right to be drafted into the army. In addition, the "Tolerance Tax," a special Jewish tax, so-called because with it the Jews bought the gentiles' tolerance to allow them to remain in Hungary, was raised by fifty percent.

But this was not enough. The government spread its concerns to interfere with traditional Jewish life. For example, in order to get married, one had to prove that one had completed one's learning in a "normal school," where secular topics were studied.

All of this flowed out of a mixture of the traditional anti-Semitic passions and the Enlightenment policy of assimilating the Jews.

Meanwhile, in France, the center of Enlightenment agitation, Napoleon Bonaparte was convening a meeting that offered great hopes to the Jews, but whose concealed intention was inimical to them.

Napoleon Bonaparte, the great general and liberator of Europe, had proclaimed the convening, for the first time since the dispersal of the Jews, of a Napoleon's *Sanhedrin*!

Like the original great *Sanhedrin*, this *Sanhedrin* too had seventy-one members. This *Sanhedrin* would make official the stance of the Jews on a variety of social issues. Earlier in the year, an Assembly of Jewish Notables had pledged itself to such declarations such as that the Jews viewed French gentiles as their brothers and France as their native land, which they would defend and whose laws they obeyed. The Assembly had also been asked more sensitive questions on topics such as the Jewish attitude toward intermarriage. The Jews stated their position in a language that was extremely conciliatory and tended to support Napoleon's Enlightenment beliefs.

Leaders were now chosen from all bands on the spectrum of Jewish belief and practice, from the very Orthodox to the most outspokenly liberal. Napoleon hoped that these men would be universally viewed as the legitimate spokesmen for the Jewish people. By pledging themselves to positions that weakened Jewish autonomy, these leaders, Napoleon hoped, would pave the way for Jewish assimilation.

The senior rabbi of this mock Napoleon's *Sanhedrin* was a Rabbi David Sinzheim, a distinguished rabbi who had known Rabbi Sofer in Frankfurt.

After the seven meetings of the *Sanhedrin* were concluded and the convocation dissolved, Rabbi Sinzheim sent letters to various Torah authorities explaining his position and the role he had played in the *Sanhedrin*. One of the rabbis to whom he wrote was Rabbi Sofer.

131

Rabbi Sofer wrote back, stating that there was an obligation to explain the ways of Torah to non-Jews, in accordance with their ability to understand. Rabbi Sofer praised Rabbi Sinzheim for his adroit handling of the *Sanhedrin* proceedings. Rabbi David Sinzheim's explanation of Jewish positions was both acceptable to the French and in consonance with authentic Jewish teachings.

A year later, in 1808, Napoleon revealed his more ruthless side when, under the influence of anti-Semitic pressure, he delivered an anti-Jewish decree, in which he severely limited the conditions of Jewish equality. This ruling became known as the "Infamous Decree."

Meanwhile, Rabbi Sofer set about establishing himself in Pressburg. Rabbi Sofer's official tasks in Pressburg were to teach Torah and to act as judge. In return, he was given a salary, a place to live, full support for eight *yeshivah* students and partial support for another sixteen students.

This Chasam Sofer's *yeshivah* soon grew to be the most important and well-known *yeshivah* in all of western Europe. It was attended by hundreds of students from Hungary, Germany, Bohemia, Moravia, Poland and Lithuania. Rabbi Sofer won the love of all of his students, and when they left the *yeshivah*, they spread across Europe, taking his influence with them. To support the many more students who attended his *yeshivah* beyond the basic support that the community had pledged itself to, Rabbi Sofer set up committees to support Torah scholars who learned full-time—in particular, young *yeshivah* students.

But Rabbi Sofer did not confine his task of strengthening Torah observance and Torah learning to an elite few in his *yeshivah*. He enacted regulations that would ensure that every Jew in Pressburg have the opportunity for Torah learning. Rabbi Sofer decreed that groups of people should meet to learn Torah. Each group would be led by a Torah scholar who would teach them at least a minimum of *Chumash* with *Rashi*, *Mishnah* and basic *halachos*. He set minimal amounts of time per day that every person, be he scholar or layman, must set aside to learn Torah. He gave more talks to the community than rabbis customarily did.

In addition to this, Rabbi Sofer involved himself with all aspects of community life. He made sure that the *shochtim* and the *mohelim* were competent. He officiated at weddings and burials so conscientiously that he was even called back from vacations to conduct weddings.

Rabbi Sofer had an open house, and a constant stream of visitors came to see him, to learn from him and to ask for his blessings and advice. Rabbi Sofer greeted his visitors pleasantly. He spoke with Torah scholars on their level and with simple people on their level. He helped rich and poor, honored and humble, doing as much as he could for all of them.

One time, when someone was speaking publicly against him, Rabbi Sofer commented, "I'm really quite surprised, because I don't remember having done him a favor. Usually, people repay good with evil. But since I never did anything for him, why is he treating me so badly?"

As a result of Rabbi Sofer's energy and altruism, Pressburg became a center of strong and revitalized Jewish life. Pressburg also became financially more secure, and the people attributed this to Rabbi Sofer's influence.

Rabbi Sofer's authority continued to spread beyond the boundaries of his city. Rabbis from various cities turned to him for help. Government officials came to him to clarify points of Jewish law. Even when he went on vacation, Rabbi Sofer's mail would be forwarded to him, and he would immediately answer the most urgent letters.

There were, however, occasions when Rabbi Sofer's authority was not respected. In one instance, a man named

Wolf Kammern, a real estate manager, raised the rents of a number of houses under the influence of the woman who owned the property and whom he worked for. This was in defiance of a Jewish regulation that had been in force since 1714. When Rabbi Sofer told this man to retract these raises, the man followed his employer's suggestion and summoned Rabbi Sofer to the gentile courts.

In another instance, the neighboring town of Jergen suffered a terrible fire that destroyed, among other things, its Torah scrolls. The leaders of Jergen asked the community of Pressburg to lend them a Torah scroll. Rabbi Sofer ruled that this request was legitimate and should be acceded to. But although the people of Pressburg were willing to send material aid, they did not agree to send the scroll.

Subsequent events persuaded many people that both these instances of disobeying Rabbi Sofer's will met with punishment from Heaven.

France was still stretching out across the European continent. Napoleon Bonaparte was making his bid to become a world-leader on a scale not attempted since, perhaps, the days of Alexander the Great. In 1809, war broke out between France and Austria, where Pressburg was located. Rifles, sabers, cutlasses, artillery and grapeshot—all these became part of the new vocabulary. These tools of war would be used, Napoleon declared, in the service of enlightenment.

21

State of Siege

"AHHHH!" RABBI SOFER'S HEAD SNAPPED UP AND HIS EYES OPENED suddenly, a look of horror on his face. He was awake. It had only been a dream—another dream of horror and destruction. Rabbi Sofer shakily wiped the cold sweat from his brow. These were not merely dreams—they were signs from Heaven. But what did they portend?

Then strange omens began taking place. In the midst of *Simchas Torah*, a lamp that had been firmly attached to the wall came crashing to the floor. A young, outstanding student who attempted to sing two songs grew flustered when he came to the verse beginning with the letter "*zayin*." Soon afterwards, this young student died suddenly.

Two distinguished community members reported to Rabbi Sofer that a loud, shrieking wail had reverberated throughout the home of one of them.

Rabbi Sofer's orphaned nephew, Shmuel Strauss, son of his sister, celebrated his *bar-mitzvah*. But just as he was about to recite his *derashah*, someone came in and announced that a man had died in the building. Since Shmuel was a *kohein*, he had to leave without delivering the talk. At the same time, Shmuel's family in Frankfurt-am-Main was celebrating the event with a family gathering. A fire broke out on the street, burning all the houses on one side of the street up to the house of the boy's grandmother and on the other side all the houses up to the house of the boy's father.

And night after night, the appalling dreams continued.

Now the omens became more serious. A freakish cold wave swept through the region. The Danube River was completely iced over. Then, the weather suddenly became mild. The ice melted, but large chunks of tons of ice dammed up the river. The river overflowed its banks and water coursed through the streets of Pressburg and surrounding villages, flooding the houses and forcing people to travel through the streets in rowboats. Many people died.

Non-Jews from the village of Uj were left homeless and streamed to Pressburg, where the Jews compassionately took them in. This warm-hearted attitude of the Jews was recognized and appreciated by the government and gentiles in general.

Still more tragic and inexplicable events occurred. A sudden storm threatened to sink a ship sailing on the Danube, then just as suddenly subsided. A prominent woman, the wife of Joseph Bettelheim, disappeared. She was discovered dead a day later in a field, unmolested, with none of her jewelry or money taken.

And Rabbi Sofer's dark and disturbing dreams continued with greater frequency and force.

The harsh winter ended. But the spring brought with it the troops of Napoleon's army. The Jews of Pressburg were sanguine, believing that Napoleon represented no threat and would soon be gone.

But Rabbi Sofer did not agree. Gathering a *minyan*, Rabbi Sofer pledged them to silence and performed a mystical *pidyon nefesh* ceremony based on the text of the Ramban, offering a sum of 541 gulden (the numerical equivalent of the word Israel) in charity in exchange for the well-being of the Jews.

On the eighteenth of *Sivan*, a Thursday night, Rabbi Sofer's foreboding were realized. With a mighty crash of artillery, Napoleon's army began its bombardment.

On *Shabbos*, Rabbi Sofer delivered a talk in which he urged the people to gain G-d's favor by supporting indigent Torah scholars.

While the people were still in the synagogue praying, a thunderous explosion rocked the building. Bombs fell through the streets, and Rabbi Sofer and his students went down into a cellar, where they learned and had *shalosh seudos*.

But this was merely a taste of things to come. The shelling consisted only of a few stray shells that had missed their targets, Austrian boats upon the Danube.

Soon afterwards, as Rabbi Sofer and his students sat in a cellar learning, the real shelling began: a direct assault on Pressburg. Like deafening thunder, the bombs burst in the city streets, shaking houses, shattering windows and exploding terrifyingly.

The sustained assault lasted throughout the day. To walk in the streets was to court death. Families cowered in cellars and children cried in terror at the whistle and explosion of the artillery.

But miraculously, not one Jewish home was damaged by the bombardment.

Rabbi Sofer again performed a *pidyon nefesh* ceremony, this time in public.

Soon afterwards, a delegate from the nearby community of Jergen arrived and urged Rabbi Sofer to take refuge there. Rabbi Sofer was inclined to do so, both because his family urged him to and because he had had numerous dreams in which he had been forced to flee Pressburg. By leaving now, he considered, he would be putting behind him that disturbing prophecy.

But many people of Pressburg's community prevailed upon him to remain, and Rabbi Sofer allowed them to persuade him. Soon after, however, when it became apparent that Napoleon was preparing for a major attack, these community leaders changed their minds and urged Rabbi Sofer to flee, and he and his family made their way to Jergen.

There in Jergen, Rabbi Sofer continued to teach his students who had accompanied him. The majority of students remained in Pressburg and so the *yeshivah* remained in operation.

The days passed peacefully, and people began claiming that Napoleon would not attack, after all. Many Jews were so bad-off that they had to sleep in the field, and they were eager to return to their homes. But Rabbi Sofer disagreed with their assessment, and decided to remain in Jergen. He did start out for Pressburg on the day preceding the first of *Tammuz*, to deliver a sermon to the people encouraging them to engage in acts of repentance and loving-kindness. But mysteriously, Rabbi Sofer's carriage overturned and shattered, very nearly injuring him. Rabbi Sofer saw this as a sign from Heaven, and he remained in Jergen.

Soon the bombardment of Pressburg began again. Although many gentiles were killed, there was miraculously no damage or injury in the Jewish quarter. In the following days, there was a lull in the fighting, and Rabbi Sofer returned to Pressburg, this time staying with his family in a house that had a cellar.

Although again many Jews believed that the danger was over, Rabbi Sofer was still ill-at-ease.

On the ninth of *Tammuz*, Rabbi Sofer delivered an important talk to the community, explaining the meaning of the events that they had been living through. The fact that the Jews of Pressburg had thus far escaped unharmed was a miracle, Rabbi Sofer said. But a still greater miracle was the fact that Pressburg had come under siege in the first place. The entire campaign made no military sense whatsoever, and could best be explained as G-d's warning to the Jews to improve their actions. Because G-d had sent His warning in the form of weapons, Jews should repent in those matters that are compared to weapons—in particular, to arrows. The sin of impure thoughts is compared to an arrow. Jews must therefore improve their level of modesty. Men and women should not gather in mixed groups, in parks or in homes. Fathers should urge their daughters to dress modestly. Slander and talebearing are compared to an arrow. Jews must guard their tongues. Finally, shaving with a razor is indirectly compared to an arrow. Those Jews who had taken up this practice must desist from it.

Rabbi Sofer also urged the Jews to engage in additional Torah study and to rebuild the destroyed walls of the cemetery, in order to gain the merit of the holy men buried there.

Finally, Rabbi Sofer spoke directly about a sore point that had been on many people's minds. Many people believed that, as their leader, Rabbi Sofer had a responsibility to remain with them. His flight to Jergen, they believed, was a betrayal of their trust. Rabbi Sofer discussed this candidly and at length. At the end of his talk, the people were reconciled to him and their bitter feelings dissolved.

On the thirteenth of *Tammuz*, a new artillery attack began. But again, G-d's saving Hand was evident. Although many gentiles were killed, there was not a single Jewish fatality. And despite the many shells that hit Jewish homes, not one fire broke out and there was only minor damage.

But the Jewish quarter could not continue to be miraculously protected. The next morning, a new artillery attack began, raining destruction on the streets. By the end of the attack, only four houses, including the synagogue and Rabbi Sofer's home, were left standing. Again, Rabbi Sofer took refuge in Jergen.

The next night began the most fierce bombardment of all. What bombs did not destroy, fire burned. And what the fire did not ruin was carried off by looters. It seemed that the destruction was universal.

At that time, Wolf Kammern was shot in the leg. Without anesthetics, he had to undergo a series of harrowing operations. He confessed his sins, and repented for having unfairly raised the Jews' rent. Soon afterwards, he died.

The entire city of Pressburg was now in desperate straits. People were homeless and penniless. The Parliament itself was blown to bits.

The Jewish community gathered its Torah scrolls and brought them to Jergen for safe-keeping. Rabbi Sofer saw in this retribution for the Pressburg community's earlier refusal to lend Jergen a Torah scroll in Jergen's time of need.

Again there were rumors of an imminent cease-fire. Again, Rabbi Sofer was distrustful of such a belief, and again he was proven to be correct. Renewed fighting broke out.

But finally, at the beginning of the month of *Av*, a cease-fire went into effect and Rabbi Sofer returned to Pressburg. Still, the city's troubles were far from over. Napoleon had forced the Austrians to agree to pay ruinous fines, and the Jews would have to provide a substantial portion of them. Much property had been destroyed and fires continued to rage. Jews had been unable to earn money during the war, and now inflation raged and made it impossible for many people to support themselves. Many Jews were left homeless and impoverished.

Jews engaged in money-exchanging to service the soldiers who wished to convert their foreign gold and silver coins into the local currency. Even young boys walked through the streets carrying large bags bulging with coins. But this activity aroused the ire of anti-Semites. The government informed the Jews that anti-Jewish feeling was growing and Rabbi Sofer delivered a stern talk. He demanded that all the money-changing activity stop. He was particularly angry that young boys, who should be learning Torah, were being used in such a way.

During the entire course of the siege, Rabbi Sofer had continued delivering his Torah lessons daily. But his *yeshivah* was in shambles. Before the war had broken out, three hundred students had been learning in the Chasam Sofer's *yeshivah*. Now, a month and a half later, only a handful of students remained.

Throughout the siege and in its aftermath, Rabbi Sofer played a strong role in leading the community, in settling disputes and in keeping up the spirits of the people. As he had in earlier crises, Rabbi Sofer showed himself to be a strong and principled leader.

One incident that occurred in the aftermath of the destruction involved a coincidence so unlikely that attribution to Divine Providence seemed the most credible interpretation.

Peasants scoured the battlefields where the bodies of thousands of soldiers lay. These peasants looted the dead soldiers of their weaponry and sold them to Jewish arms dealers. One of these dealers was a man named Mordechai Oberbreit.

He and a partner were arrested by the French soldiers as they were transporting the armaments to Budapest for the use of the Austrian army. Both they and others narrowly escaped receiving the death penalty, and the Jewish community itself was in great danger of attack by anti-Semites as a result of their activities.

Soon afterwards, these two men had a falling-out regarding how to split their profits. They brought their dispute to the Pressburg *beis din*, which handed down its decision. The man in whose favor the *beis din* had decided reported this to the military court. Although Rabbi Sofer hadn't been a signatory to the *beis din's* decision, the French authorities summoned him to a court martial on the grounds that he was a member of the *beis din*. He was accused of being a spy on behalf of the Budapest army, and summoned to stand trial.

On the night preceding the court martial, Rabbi Sofer could not sleep. He wanted to flee Pressburg, but the community leaders dissuaded him from such a move. Instead, they collected ten thousand gulden with which to bribe the prosecutors. They could hardly expect justice there. Court martial proceedings were quick and capricious, and could as easily rule for death as for life.

The next day, when Rabbi Sofer entered the court martial room, he stepped into the middle of a circle. Surrounding him were the officers who would try him, each holding his naked sword in his hand.

When Rabbi Sofer saw this, he grew pale. Would they be so murderous as to slay him even as he stood before them defending himself?

"Calm down, Rabbi," said the general in charge of the proceedings. "No one will hurt you. This is merely the custom of a court martial proceeding, in order to frighten the defendant." The general returned his sword to its scabbard. "Gentlemen, return your swords!" he ordered, and the other officers put away their blades of steel.

"Your name, for the record?" asked the general.

"Rabbi Moshe Sofer."

The general halted, then he continued. "Of?"

"Chief Rabbi of Pressburg."

"No, before that. What is your native city?"

"Frankfurt-am-Main."

The general's face grew strangely excited. There was a wild tone in his voice. "Come with me into the other room, Rabbi. Officers, remain here until we return."

As soon as Rabbi Sofer and the general entered the other room, the general closed the door behind him. "Rabbi Sofer!" he said, going up close to Rabbi Sofer and looking him straight in the face. "Have I grown so old that you no longer recognize me? I am Bios de Monfort!"

"Bios de Monfort, whom I taught German in Mainz?" Rabbi Sofer exclaimed.

"Yes, Rabbi Sofer, over thirty years ago, when you were a young boy and I was just an enlisted officer. But look at us now. I am a general, and you are a rabbi—a Chief Rabbi. You don't know how much you did for me with your lessons. You remember how we used to talk about the meaning of life? You opened up a whole world for me: the world of the Jews' Torah. You know, I have never forgotten those talks. They have remained with me until this day."

"But what shall happen now, my dear General Monfort? I am on trial for my life."

"Tell me, what really happened?"

"These two men came to my court and just told in general terms about a business disagreement that they had. They never mentioned that they were dealing in arms. My court would never have ruled on their case if it had known that. I promise you, in the name of our old friendship, that this is the truth!"

"Do not worry, Rabbi Sofer. I am with you. Let us go back out to the court martial. State your case carefully, and I will do all I can to see that not a hair on your head is injured."

143

The two men returned to the trial room. General Monfort nodded to Rabbi Sofer. "Begin your testimony," he said in a dry voice.

Rabbi Sofer cogently stated the facts of the matter. When he was finished with his presentation, the officers convened and, under the influence of General Monfort, acquitted Rabbi Sofer of all the charges against him.

In the following years, the Jews' situation remained precarious. A fire swept through Pressburg in 1810, again reducing many Jews to homelessness. But with the lingering end of the sufferings brought about by this combat began the conflict that would engage Rabbi Sofer for the rest of his life: the clash between Torah and non-Torah values.

No battle is worth the fight and the sacrifice if it is not being waged on behalf of a worthy cause. Rabbi Sofer's cause was Torah, and his first priority was not to fight the forces against Torah but to strengthen those dedicated to it and to widen its influence among its adherents.

22

The Great Yeshivah

"OH—EXCUSE ME, I'LL COME BACK LATER."

"No, please, come in, come in. Are those letters you have for me?"

"Yes, Rabbi Sofer. But I don't want to interrupt you in the middle of your teaching."

"That's quite all right. Thank you very much."

Having delivered the letters, the messenger backed out of the room, throwing an apologetic look at Rabbi Sofer and the students who sat about him at the long table.

"Ah! An interesting letter, this one," Rabbi Sofer said. "I will read it to you. Listen carefully." Rabbi Sofer read a letter that contained a complex *halachic* question. The caliber of the question made it clear that the letter's author was an accomplished Torah scholar.

"Now, my students, does anyone know who wrote this?"

No one responded.

"I will tell you. When I was still a boy living in Frankfurt-am-Main, there was a horse-seller who had a young unmarried man in his early twenties working for him. I'd see this young man every once in a while. He was an ignoramus, a feeble character who was wasting his life away. All he did was ride through the streets on errands.

"One day when I was walking in the street, he galloped by, and his horse threw him. While he was lifting himself up from the ground, I went over to him and rebuked him for living such a meaningless life. A Jew who can think of nothing more than riding back and forth on his horse!

"I told him that he should be learning Torah. I said that if he agreed to learn, I would learn together with him.

"He came with me to the *beis midrash*, and learned with me a while. Soon, he changed himself around completely and devoted himself to learning Torah and serving G-d.

"It is that former ignoramus who wrote me this letter that I just read you."

Rabbi Sofer's students were the most promising young scholars. The greatest rabbis sent their sons to his *yeshivah* to learn. Rabbi Sofer often admonished them, and in particular, the more talented ones among them, not to grow haughty, but to keep a clear perspective on themselves and their accomplishments. Bright students are often praised excessively in order to encourage them. The result at times is that these students feel themselves immeasurably superior to any Jew who is not learning in a *yeshivah*. In addition, they take a cruel pleasure in vanquishing weaker students in Talmudic reasoning.

With such a story did Rabbi Sofer teach his students that all Jews have a portion of the Torah and all Jews have the potential to become learned.

Rabbi Sofer loved his thousands of students dearly. But he

held himself back from demonstrating his love for them. As a result, his students reciprocated his feelings with love combined with awe. In consequence of Rabbi Sofer's warm but firm approach, very few of his students left the path of Torah. Once Rabbi Sofer confided to a colleague that although he loved his students very much, he never let the financial supporters of the *yeshivah* be aware of this, and never asked any favors for them. His reason was, he said, that if such a supporter ever got angry at him, he would not take his anger out on a blameless student.

In addition, because Rabbi Sofer loved his students the way a father loves his children, they grew to love one another like brothers.

When he taught, Rabbi Sofer explicated the material clearly, and always made sure that the students learned the actual method of learning Talmud; *halachic* decision that the *Gemara* passage they were learning led to. He once wrote, "One must know how Rav and Shmuel themselves discussed the *halachah* when a case came before them, and what conclusion they came to."

With such an approach, it would be very hard for a student to fool himself into thinking that he truly understood a subject, unless he could clearly recall the definitive *halachic* ruling.

Students at Rabbi Sofer's Chasam Sofer *Yeshivah* had to undergo a rigorous system of examinations. In many yeshivas, a student could attend a *shiur* for years and never once have to give an account of himself. When a *rebbe* allowed students to remain in a *shiur* without demanding that they demonstrate their understanding, this provided the *rebbe* with an excuse not to make an effort to explain himself clearly.

But in the *yeshivah* of Pressburg, Rabbi Sofer demanded that the students be held accountable—which meant that he also held himself accountable for presenting the material to them lucidly. A month before the end of the *z'man*, Rabbi Sofer told his students to review everything they had learned over the last half year. He then tested them on all the material.

Rabbi Sofer did not feel the need to dazzle his students with his brilliance. When he began to teach a topic, he went over it so slowly and so carefully that it appeared that he had never seen the words before. Before beginning to teach, he would repeat a line of the *Mishnah* a number of times, following the place with his finger. He did this whether learning alone or in public. He taught very carefully and very precisely, making sure that the slowest student understood the topic. To Rabbi Sofer, all the students in his *shiur* were important, not just the two or three brightest.

In addition, Rabbi Sofer encouraged his students to listen to his words analytically and critically. Whereas it is the teacher's responsibility to say everything he has thought of, he would tell his students, it is their responsibility to analyze what they had heard and to choose the best for themselves. He taught his students to become emotionally and intellectually independent.

In his youth, Rabbi Sofer had been quite fond of the brilliant method of *pilpul*. Afterwards, however, he abandoned this method, preferring instead a simple approach. At times, Rabbi Sofer would pose an apparent contradiction in the *Rambam* to his students. Then he would solve the problem in two ways. First, he would employ a complex *pilpul* to resolve the contradiction, and then he would resolve it through a simple analysis without bringing in any extraneous material.

"Which answer did you prefer?" Rabbi Sofer would then ask.

Invariably, most of the students would reply that they had preferred the *pilpul* method. It was dazzling, clever, an intellectual *tour de force*.

But Rabbi Sofer would say, "The *pilpul* answer was more clever. But the second answer was true. And remember, students, there is nothing in the whole world more important than truth."

In his later years, when Rabbi Sofer was a father and his children were growing up, he once sat at a meal and related to his children all the many good traits of Rabbi Akiva Eiger, their grandfather. He told them about Rabbi Akiva Eiger's piety, his holiness, his modesty, his intense Torah learning and his careful keeping of *halachah*. "May you as well inherit and realize these good traits," Rabbi Sofer blessed his children.

Rabbi Sofer's son, Shimon Sofer, asked him, "Father, haven't you forgotten to mention Grandfather's depth and sharpness in learning?"

Rabbi Sofer replied, "I did not forget, son. I left that out deliberately. When it comes to the method of learning Torah, I would prefer that you learn from me and not from my father-in-law. I, thank G-d, have a better method of learning than he. One must know how the Talmudic argument is built. One must know the entire passage clearly and what the *halachic* outcome is. This is absolutely vital if you are going to take responsibility for making *halachic* decisions. This is what is called good learning."

Rabbi Sofer felt that sometimes *pilpul* was an attempt to solve what was actually a copying mistake in a manuscript. In one of his *teshuvos*, Rabbi Sofer commented, "In my humble opinion, the entire *pilpul* discussion here is mistaken. Rather, a small correction must be made in the text."

Another time, Rabbi Sofer advised a student, "Set aside the works of the *acharonim* with their deep *pilpul* and complex analysis. Instead, fill your mind with the works of the *rishonim*, for everyone needs a master of *halachah*."

Rabbi Sofer encouraged his students to learn the Talmud

in order and not to skip from one section to another. He wrote, "The Torah scholars of the age must be rebuked for teaching simultaneously and superficially. Worse than this are those who skip about, not learning entire tractates but a little from one and a little from another."

Rabbi Sofer felt that students should cover ground in their learning without getting entangled in complex arguments. To one student, he wrote, "Be strong and learn at least a few pages of *Gemara* every day. Then review it without the *pilpul* that people are accustomed to."

Rabbi Sofer stressed both covering ground and review of the material. He was very strict that his students constantly reviewed the material that they learned. He himself reviewed any lesson that he taught four times during the day.

Rabbi Sofer used whatever means necessary to bring clarity to his lessons. He engaged in practical experiments to determine the measurements of a *reviis hakos*, a *kezayis* and a *kebeyah*. He tested kernels of wheat and other grains to determine how they became leavened. In the *shiurim* of some other *rebbes*, it was possible to learn through an entire *sugya* without understanding the specific facts that one was discussing. One could get by simply by understanding the logic of the arguments. Rabbi Sofer would never allow such a thing in his *yeshivah*. He even owned a number of human anatomical figures that could be taken apart to demonstrate the way the organs of the body operate, and he would use these to help illumine passages in the *Gemara*.

Rabbi Sofer felt that it was quite important that his students use all avenues necessary to understand the Torah, including such topics as geometry, algebra, astronomy, anatomy and physics—topics that he himself was an expert in. At one time, he considered writing a book that would explain all these topics cogently. This would save his students from having to turn to non-Jewish authors to learn the material.

However, at that time, *Sefer Habris*, a textbook on the sciences, appeared. Rabbi Sofer instructed his students to study that book. He told them, "You and I must be thankful to the author of *Sefer Habris*, for he has saved me a lot of time that I can now devote to learning Torah, since I do not have to set aside any time to write such a book myself."

The *yeshivah* of Pressburg was innovative in a number of other ways. It offered a program on public speaking, so that graduates of the *yeshivah* would be able to effectively relate to others. The *yeshivah* also offered educational projects in conjunction with the city's laymen. But Rabbi Sofer's students were taught that "All Jews are responsible for one another" and that, as Torah students, they had an obligation to share their learning with all Jews.

In addition, Rabbi Sofer's *yeshivah* taught *Tanach* and grammar, topics that were neglected in other *yeshivos*.

Rabbi Sofer would preface every *shiur* with a quarter hour lesson from *Chovas Halevovos*, including the translator's introduction, as well as the *Sha'ar Hayichud* together with its preface. Almost all of Rabbi Sofer's *mussar* and personal habits were based upon this *sefer*. Once, Rabbi Mordechai Banet told Rabbi Sofer, "People say that you are a living *Chovas Halevovos*."

Rabbi Sofer urged his students to study this *sefer* and use it to forge their own path in serving G-d. Rabbi Sofer also told his students to learn *Menoras Hamaor*, because it contained many *aggados*. (Some students tended to neglect the learning of *Aggadah*.) In his later years, Rabbi Sofer learned *Menoras Hamaor* together with his own daughters.

Rabbi Sofer also encouraged his students to familiarize themselves with works that contained historical information such as *Megillas Taanis*, *Yossiphon*, *Tzemach David* (by Rabbi David Ganz, a student of the Rema), *Seder Hadoros* (by Rabbi Yechiel Halperin, early 1700s) and others.

With love and authority, analysis and clarity, and unrelenting diligence, Rabbi Sofer taught Torah and inculcated it in his thousands of students, in the laymen of Pressburg and in the many who turned to him from many regions of Europe.

23

The Ways of Greatness

ON A TYPICAL DAY, RABBI SOFER AROSE SWIFTLY FROM BED AT FOUR in the morning (on both weekdays and *Shabbos*; he never went to sleep earlier than midnight).

He washed his hands, said the morning blessings and then recited the blessing over the Torah. Then, at dawn, he went to an unheated *mikveh*. He then put on his *tallis* and *tefillin* and quickly walked to the *beis midrash*.

In the summer, he *davened Shacharis* at six o'clock in the morning, and in the winter, at dawn (both on weekdays and *Shabbos*).

Rabbi Sofer prayed very slowly and with great intensity, often breaking into tears. Once in his youth, his fellow students had teased him that in the time that it took him to pray, they were able to learn a paragraph of the *Shulchan Aruch* with the commentary of the *Magen Avraham*. He replied, "The Talmud states that when a person prays at length, he is given long life. If that is so, then I will have a long life and I will have the time to go through many paragraphs of the *Shulchan Aruch*."

While reciting the *Shmoneh Esrei*, Rabbi Sofer stood perfectly still. Only his lips moved, but one could hear nothing.

Before each prayer (including *Maariv*), Rabbi Sofer gave charity.

He did not change the order of the prayers at all. Although he prayed from the *siddur* of the Ari, he was very careful to pray *nussach Ashkenaz*. Privately he would say "*morid hatal*" and, at *Minchah*, "*sim shalom*"; but when he led the prayers on a *yahrzeit*, he prayed like everyone else. Rabbi Sofer was careful not to change even the tune of the prayers.

Rabbi Sofer generally prayed in the same place that he taught.

After finishing the majority of the prayers, Rabbi Sofer learned the *Tur Orach Chaim*, with the *Magen Avraham*, while still in his *tallis* and *tefillin*. (Two exceptions were on Fridays or on days when he served as a *mohel*. Also, before a holiday, *Purim*, *Chanukah* or *Tishah b'Av*, he learned the laws of the upcoming day.)

Rabbi Sofer now drank coffee. The coffee was so hot that Rabbi Sofer could only sip it. Nevertheless, he recited an after-blessing.

Afterwards, Rabbi Sofer took off his *tefillin*, put on *Rabbeinu Tam tefillin* and completed his prayers.

Then he went home and ate a breakfast of bread, in accordance with the Talmud's emphasis on a proper morning meal.

Rabbi Sofer then prepared his lesson for two hours until ten o'clock. Then, he went to the women's section, where he taught his *shiur*.

Not a day of the year went by that Rabbi Sofer did not teach Torah (with the exception of *Tishah b'Av*).

At the beginning of every *z'man*, Rabbi Sofer prefaced his lesson with words of *Aggadah* and *mussar*, always making sure to end with a positive comment. Between *Pesach* and *Shavuos*, Rabbi Sofer taught his students *Shavuos*. During *Adar*, he taught Megillah.

In the winter, Rabbi Sofer taught in the *beis midrash*, where the humidity was so bad that it was sometimes impossible to light candles. But in the summer, he taught in the synagogue next to the *aron kodesh*. After he prefaced the *shiur* with a lesson from *Chovos Halevovos*, students who were mourners recited the *kaddish derabanan* in unison.

When he taught, Rabbi Sofer exhibited a great deal of joy.

During the *shiur*, whenever Rabbi Sofer proposed some logical reasoning or resolution of a problem, the students immediately reviewed his words among themselves, and his best students discussed it with him. (Also, when Rabbi Sofer spoke in the synagogue, whether on *halachah* or *Aggadah*, the congregation would review his words while he paused.)

When he returned home from teaching his *shiur*, he went over the letters that had come in the mail. He ate lunch in his room alone, continuing his replies to the letters.

Rabbi Sofer ate bland food. If he found something especially tasty, he would not eat it. Once, he was told that Rabbi Banet only ate a minimum amount of food. Rabbi Sofer commented, "Not to eat for the sake of Heaven is not such a great trick. A greater accomplishment is eating for the sake of Heaven." The beverages that Rabbi Sofer drank were so hot that no one else could taste them. Rabbi Sofer persisted in this practice even when doctors asked him not to. Even when he ate alone, Rabbi Sofer recited the grace after meals holding a glass of wine.

After marrying his second wife, Seril, Rabbi Sofer began

155

the habit of taking a one or two-hour nap after lunch. He did so not because he felt the need to but because on his wedding day, Rabbi Akiva Eiger, his father-in-law, had requested this of him.

After his nap, Rabbi Sofer wrote answers to urgent letters. He only answered non-urgent letters on Wednesday and Thursday, when he did not teach an *iyun shiur* (a deeper analysis of the Talmud passage). He would not reply twice to a correspondent regarding the same *halachah*, even if the correspondent wrote back to discuss a point.

Rabbi Sofer taught his *iyun shiur* three times during the week. On Wednesday, the students reviewed their lessons and on Thursday before noon they were tested. That day, Rabbi Sofer himself reviewed the material with them four times.

In addition to his regular *iyun shiurim*, which were about important topics, Rabbi Sofer also taught the *Gemara* page-by-page, completing one *masechta* and immediately starting the next.

Between *Minchah* and *Maariv*, Rabbi Sofer learned with his students. On Sunday, Monday and Tuesday, he learned *Tur*, *Yoreh Deah* with the commentary of the *Shach*. On Wednesdays, Rabbi Sofer wrote down all of his original Torah thoughts that he had taught the students. On Wednesdays and Thursdays, Rabbi Sofer learned the weekly *parshah* with *Rashi* and *Ramban*.

At his home, a student would read out of a Talmud while he listened.

Rabbi Sofer's house was always open to people to discuss Torah with him, except for when he was teaching. Even so, if someone wanted to come in and a student wanted to keep him out, Rabbi Sofer rebuked him, "Let him in. Who knows how urgent his question may be?"

On Thursday night, he came to the *beis midrash* at

midnight to recite *tikkun chatzos* with his students, and he mourned deeply over the destruction of the Beis Hamikdash.

On Friday morning after *Shacharis*, while still wearing the *tefillin* of Rabbeinu Tam, Rabbi Sofer went over the *parshah* twice with the *targum*. He taught the *parshah* with *Rashi* to his students. On Friday morning until noon, Rabbi Sofer reviewed all the material that he had taught that week. He again learned the *parshah* with *Rashi* and *Ramban*. He also wrote down his novel Torah thoughts on *Aggadah*.

Rabbi Sofer highly praised the Ramban's commentary on the *Chumash*. He felt a special affinity with the writings of the Ramban, and studied them with special diligence.

On Friday, Rabbi Sofer didn't have a full meal. Although he had a light breakfast, he skipped lunch.

On Friday afternoon, Rabbi Sofer bathed in an extremely hot bath, into which the man in charge of the *mikveh* put herbs to strengthen his arteries. He then went to the *mikveh*. He immersed himself ten times and changed into his *Shabbos* clothes there.

Rabbi Sofer prayed *Maariv* early on Friday evening, but he stayed in the synagogue until after nightfall. Everyone repeated *Shema* together with him, and he spoke about the *parshah*.

After *Mizmor Shir* was recited on Friday night, Rabbi Sofer smelled spices. (He also did this every holiday before *borchu*, including *Yom Kippur*.)

When he came home, Rabbi Sofer blessed his children— either those whom he raised or, later on, his own.

At home, Rabbi Sofer did not say *Shalom Aleichem*, *Yehi Ratzon* nor *Azamin Bishvachin*. He only recited *Aishes Chayil* as well as Ibn Ezra's Tzam'ah Nafshi. He praised this song very highly as being full of *Kabbalistic* wisdom. He said that there was no doubt whatsoever that Ibn Ezra had been inspired from heaven when he had composed this poem. He said the first part of *Kiddush* standing and the blessing while sitting.

On Friday evening, Rabbi Sofer did not dip the bread in salt. During the meal, all the *zemiros* printed in the *siddur* were sung at his table.

Both during the evening and day meals, Rabbi Sofer learned from *Rabbeinu Bachya's* commentary on the *parshah* between courses.

At least two students ate at his table, and in addition, he paid someone else to invite the other students.

On Friday night, Rabbi Sofer reviewed all his lessons of the past week. In his room were two lamps that burned until dawn. He learned with three students. One looked on with him, and two others learned from a second *sefer*.

On Friday night, Rabbi Sofer slept in his clothes.

On *Shabbos* morning after *Mussaf*, Rabbi Sofer learned Tur on the laws of *Shabbos*. Then he delivered a lesson on the *parshah*.

He made *Kiddush* immediately after the prayers. Because he couldn't drink wine on an empty stomach, he had someone else in his family make *Kiddush* for him.

If Rabbi Sofer had to give a talk on a *Shabbos*, he composed it in his mind at this time before going over to the large synagogue.

If Rabbi Sofer did not have guests for the day meal, he would learn until lunchtime. In the afternoon, Rabbi Sofer took a nap. In the summer, he would then learn *Pirkei Avos* with the members of the *chevrah kaddisha* until *Minchah* was recited in the synagogue. He did not daven *Minchah* then. Instead, all the members of his family came to him to talk, because he had so little time to speak with them during the week. Then he davened *Minchah*.

He ate *shalosh seudos* at home with his close colleagues and a few students. He made the blessing on the bread and his servant distributed bread to everyone. He ate a little piece of fish and the servant passed out the rest of the fish to the others. Then Rabbi Sofer gave out wine to everyone and said *L'Chaim*. The others raised their goblets, all made out of silver.

He then taught *Aggadah* and *mussar*. Sometimes he would teach *halachah*.

The others would then sing his song, *Keil Mistateir*.

Grace was made on a cup of wine. The person who led the grace drank from the cup, even though night had already fallen.

In later years, before *Havdalah* was made in the *beis midrash*, Rabbi Sofer blessed his sons. He recited the song, *Hamavdil*. After *Shabbos*, Rabbi Sofer learned the Rambam's *Yad Hachazokoh*.

Rabbi Sofer went out of his way to beautify his observance of the *mitzvos* by performing them in the most complete way possible.

For instance, even though he had purchased the Torah scroll written by Rabbi Nassan Adler for a high price , he also fulfilled the *mitzvah* of writing a Torah scroll himself by hiring an expert scribe, Rabbi Zusman Sofer, to write one. Rabbi Sofer taught this man the special intentions and secrets of the letters to have in mind when writing this Torah scroll.

One afternoon, when Rabbi Zusman left Rabbi Sofer's room, he saw some Torah scholars, and he told them, "Thank G-d, I now know the alphabet."

"What are you talking about? You are a learned man!"

Rabbi Zusman explained that Rabbi Sofer was teaching him the intentions to have in mind when writing the letters in the Torah scroll.

Rabbi Sofer bought utensils of precious silver to adorn the Torah scroll as well.

Rabbi Sofer performed all *mitzvos* with great enthusiasm, and paid for the most beautiful way of performing the act.

Rabbi Sofer walked with his eyes lowered, and he greeted others before they greeted him. He stood before older, respected people. He was very careful not to have Torah scholars do anything for him.

He never cursed anyone, and he would rebuke anyone who did so, even if it was for the sake of Heaven.

Rabbi Sofer was very generous with his money, especially if it were to be spent to sanctify G-d's name. He always gave twenty percent of his salary to charity. He helped support a number of Torah scholars with weekly payments, as well as to help rabbis in various towns whom he knew were suffering financially. He also did a great deal to help his students with their material needs.

Rabbi Sofer's hand never went below his waistline. No one except Rabbi Sofer's servant ever saw him without his jacket on. No one in his household wore red clothing.

He was not strict if the name of a groom and father-in-law, or a bride and her mother-in-law were the same. Indeed his daughter Simche married Rabbi Moshe Tuvia Lehmann, and he also pointed out in a letter that his father was named Shmuel, which was also the name of his mother's father.

He insisted that there be instrumental music at a wedding.

He saw to it that the *peyos* of his students and people in his family reached down to the lower cheekbone .

He said that for good fortune and to find a lost object, it was good to pledge charity to the fund of Rabbi Akiva Frankfurt, who had started a charitable fund to which people donated money for the good of his soul.

24

Clash with Reform

ON *SHABBOS HAGADOL*, 5570 (1810), RABBI SOFER DELIVERED A sermon on the topic of eating beans on Pesach.

His talk had to do with a *halachic* question regarding a major issue of the day. But his talk went beyond the narrow *halachic* limits of the case. Instead, Rabbi Sofer outlined an inclusive and compelling view of Torah and tradition that provided a strong structure of commitment and support for the Torah-observant community.

But what did this have to do with beans?

Rabbi Sofer had received a letter from Rabbi Avraham of Glogau, Germany. This letter informed Rabbi Sofer of a *halachic* decision that had been given by the rabbinical council of the Westphalian Consistory. (One of Napoleon's innovations in all the lands he conquered was to order the Jews to form a central regional authority, called a *consistoire*.)

161

Many Jews had been drafted into the German armies. These soldiers had a great deal of trouble finding kosher food on *Pesach*. The rabbinical council of Westphalia ruled that they should be allowed to eat legumes, or beans.

Legumes are, of course, not leavened bread. The prohibition against eating legumes is neither Biblical nor Talmudic. It is a stricture, a fence around the law, and not something prohibited for its own sake. It is a prohibition decreed in the thirteenth century, and applied only to European Jews.

Many times in the past, when it was difficult to find kosher food on *Pesach*, the ban against eating legumes had been temporarily lifted. Therefore, this ruling by the rabbis of Westphalia was apparently standard and based on broad precedent.

However, there was a difference. The rabbinical council was headed by a Reform leader named Israel Jacobson. In his argument, Jacobson developed lines of reasoning based not on *halachah* but rather on his non-*halachic*, Reform point of view. In doing so, Jacobson turned a *halachic* ruling into an ideological weapon against the Torah.

Jacobson had been crafty. If his decision was approved, he could claim that the rabbis approved his Reform reasoning. And if it was dismissed, he could turn to the people and denounce the rabbis as cruel, narrow-minded clerics who were prepared to see Jewish soldiers starve for the sake of adhering to a rigid, irrelevant system of laws. But even more than that was involved. If this case turned into a dispute, there was the danger that the government would step in. And that could lead to troubles of various description.

Rabbi Avraham of Glogau explained all this to Rabbi Sofer in his letter. Rabbi Avraham wrote that he wished to organize a group of well-known rabbis who would work together to rescind the Reform decree. He invited Rabbi Sofer to join this group.

Rabbi Sofer's response to this crisis was both judicious and discreet.

He wrote back declining to join such a formal protest, arguing that this was a matter "where there is danger." By this, he presumably referred to the danger of meddling by anti-Semitic government officials who would welcome the opportunity to get involved, to the detriment of the Jewish cause.

In his letter and in his sermon on *Shabbos* Hagadol, Rabbi Sofer outlined his response to this question. He saw the issue not merely as one dealing with a particular case of the laws of *Pesach*. Instead, he viewed this as one example of a general attitude regarding the supreme value of tradition.

Those who allow the eating of legumes on *Pesach* do have a background of *halachic* opinion on which to rely, Rabbi Sofer acknowledged.

But Rabbi Sofer went on to ban the eating of legumes on different grounds. His whole philosophy of the importance of precedent and the wisdom of the generations was invoked in explaining why he felt that legumes (*kitniyos*) must remain forbidden. This philosophy of Judaism and tradition was to form the backbone of his battle against Reform and deeply influence Orthodox thinking and strategy to this very day.

Rabbi Sofer began by explaining that the ban against legumes was not merely a custom. Rather, it was a decree that the early authorities—the *rishonim*—had instituted for their community. The entire *Ashkenazic* community (the Jews of Western and Eastern Europe) was to be considered as a single group that had accepted this decree upon itself.

Under such circumstances, the ban against legumes constituted a vow. Such a vow could not be annulled by any group of rabbis.

G-d had given the sages the right to initiate practices and, once they were in place, they could not be abrogated. The earlier and later generations, Rabbi Sofer argued, are as intimately bound as father and son. Just as a son cannot easily annul his father's vow, so can later generations not easily uproot practices implemented by earlier sages.

In Rabbi Sofer's view of Judaism, Torah must be seen as an organic, whole and living tradition.

It is possible to look at the Torah tradition in a cold, clinical manner. One then can differentiate between various layers of law. For instance, some laws are Biblical. Others are rabbinic. Still others are rules, decrees and customs that have appeared in various communities over the passage of time and which have been cited in *halachah* collections. One can analyze the collection of this tradition and determine which laws are absolutely fundamental and which are not—which cannot be abrogated and which are seemingly ephemeral.

But Rabbi Sofer stressed that such a view of *halachah* is inadequate.

One could just as well analyze a living person by studying his various organs and parts of his body. One could determine that the heart is more important than a finger, and that the kidney is more vital than a foot. But a doctor who acted on such an understanding of the body would soon kill his patient. A doctor must understand that it is only for convenience's sake that a human being is divided into various organs. In truth, a human being is a living, integrated whole. All his different parts are inter-dependent. One cannot cause harm in one part of the body without affecting other parts of the body.

The same holds true for Torah tradition, Rabbi Sofer said. The Torah is not a set of legalisms, but a system for living. It is expressed through the living practices of Torah-observant Jewish communities. Although one could theoretically excise a custom without touching a Biblical law, in practice, excising the custom could cause unforetold injury to the entire body of Torah.

This was especially pertinent in Rabbi Sofer's day. Jewish

164

communities had been in existence in various cities and villages for hundreds of years, some even going back to the times of the *geonim*. In these communities, great Torah leaders had over the years infused the people and their way of life with a spirit of Torah that encompassed their entire lives. Even the language and nuances of daily behavior were expressions of a Torah attitude that had been inculcated for generations.

Now the forces of assimilation and Reform were coming, with no appreciation for the entirety of this way of life—in fact, often with contempt for it. They were attempting to experiment freely and subvert its hallowed ways.

The advocates of Reform did not have the right to play with the traditions of Jewish communities, lacking appreciation for the worth of that which they sought to change.

This was Rabbi Sofer's position. It was not only well-reasoned and well-structured, but it was one that touched a popular chord. The emphasis that he placed on the totality of the Torah heritage, rather than dealing with individual cases, provided a voice and philosophy for all adherents of Torah tradition. As a result, Rabbi Sofer gained immense support in Pressburg and beyond, and his argument spread and became a mainstay of the Torah defense against reform.

25

A Second Battle

1811 WAS A TROUBLED YEAR. ANOTHER FIRE SWEPT THROUGH THE Jewish community, destroying the Jewish hospital. And the economy was undermined when, responding to the fiscal troubles that the war with Napoleon had brought, King Francis devalued the currency to a fifth of what the previous value was.

People streamed to Rabbi Sofer with many questions of how this affected their *halachic* obligations in repaying debts and the like. If Reuven had borrowed a hundred gulden and now the money was worth only twenty guldens, what was he now obligated to pay back?

In general, Rabbi Sofer ruled that the governmental decree was *halachically* endorsed.

But in some cases, Rabbi Sofer argued that Jewish rule did not follow the government's ruling.

Late one night, there was a knock at Rabbi Sofer's door. The servant opened the door.

"There is a man who came to see you," he reported to Rabbi Sofer.

"At this hour? It must be urgent. Let him in."

"He is a gentile. He says his name is Anton Schmid."

"I have heard that name. Let him in."

A few moments later, a well-dressed forty-five-year-old man stepped into Rabbi Sofer's room.

"How do you do? Forgive me for intruding at this late hour."

"Not at all. I am sure that the matter is urgent or you would not have come at this time."

"That is exactly so."

"You are Anton Schmid, the well-known publisher?"

"I am flattered that your honor has heard of me."

"Non-Jewish printers generally do not publish works of Torah. We are thankful—and believe that it shall accrue to your merit."

Anton Schmid pulled a letter from his breast pocket and placed it on Rabbi Sofer's desk. "I have come to deliver this."

Rabbi Sofer glanced at the letter. "But this is a letter that I myself sent out." He ripped open the letter and glanced at the first page. "I mailed it this afternoon."

"Yes, and I had the devil of a time retrieving it."

"What is the meaning of this? Someone asked me a *halachic* question, and he is awaiting my reply."

"Rabbi Sofer, you have enemies. You have apparently been giving people advice in Jewish law that contravenes the new fiscal regulations of King Francis. Someone happened to find out that you had written a letter today dealing with the government evaluation, and he informed the government. Well, it so happens that I have sources of information as well. When I learned of this, I immediately ran out to get a hold of your letter before the government could. And at last, here it is!"

"I cannot thank you enough, Herr Schmid. One day, I will perhaps be empowered to return the favor."

In the coming years, Anton Schmid published many *sefarim*, including the *Shulchan Aruch*, as well as works of the Haskalah movement. Once, when he wanted to undertake the project of publishing the Talmud, he sought Rabbi Sofer's permission. Rabbi Sofer granted this, and so paid back the debt that he had unwittingly incurred.

At this time, advocates of the fledgling movement of assimilation were growing more active in Pressburg.

Several of these men one day paid a visit to Count Affani, a leading government official.

"Sir," said one of the men, his cheeks smooth-shaven and his large, domed forehead marked with fine wrinkles, "we are interested in opening a progressive school for our Jewish children. You know how backward the majority of the Jews are in Pressburg. In our school, we intend to teach both religious and secular topics."

"This sounds quite favorable," the count replied. "What does your chief rabbi have to say about your plan?"

The men exchanged glances. "Oh, the rabbi!" the man answered lightly. "I can assure you, Count Affani, as cultured men of the world, we do not have to trouble ourselves about him. You know the type, sir, bending over a dusty book of ancient religious conundrums, blocking the light of progress that tries in vain to shine through his window."

"What do you mean?" cried Count Affani.

The man hesitated. "I only mean, sir—"

"No, no, do not answer me. I know only too well what you mean. You want to persuade me that this chief rabbi of yours is some benighted man of no consequence. Allow me to enlighten you, gentlemen. After your chief rabbi came to

168

Pressburg, we monitored his mail for a year. We were amazed at his brilliance and at how in a mere few lines he was able to solve problems relating to state matters that our greatest legal authorities had been unable to determine for years. So I will thank you, gentlemen, not to speak ill of this great man. I believe this interview is over."

Rabbi Sofer won his battle against this school, and Count Affani's support greatly strengthened his position.

This movement of assimilation was at its core irreconcilable with Torah. The basis of Torah is faith and the awareness that there are many things beyond man's understanding: G-d Himself, the nature of miracles, of providence—that the fabric of reality is ultimately beyond human ken.

The assimilationist movement was, on the other hand, predicated on the belief in rationalism. Again and again, the scientific method, the application of pure reason, was leading to insights into the nature of reality and to great achievements.

On the basis of such insights, predictions were made—and proven correct. New technologies were proposed—and they worked. Elegant theories were propounded—and they were corroborated in a hundred ways.

Anton van Leeuwenhoek invented the microscope and discovered a hitherto undreamed-of world. The nature of electricity, leading to the use of batteries, motors and machinery was being discovered. The composition of the physical world as being composed of basic elements was being worked out, leading to a basis for the manufacture of thousands of compounds, some of which did not exist in nature. The steam engine was invented, leading to the invention of the train and other revolutionary changes in day-to-day life. The nature of the processes of the body was being worked out, leading to progress in medicine such as the practice of vaccination, thus saving hundreds of thousands of lives.

Earlier scientists had been religious men interested in the

nature of the world that G-d had wrought. But increasingly, science became a discipline preaching opposition to faith, and the rejection of anything which experimentation could not validate.

It looked to many as if the tools of science and rationalism could continue to indefinitely provide new triumphs and discoveries. Those who believed this, viewed the path of faith and piety as a fossil of a previous era. Rationalism was the lens through which all nature could be studied and understood, through which all problems and confusions could be solved. Not only in science but in all of life, rationalism would provide the answers. The proper application of rationalism would lead to universal happiness and universal well-being.

The Jews, who were beguiled by this powerful new view of the universe, found that their vision had been given a theoretical construct in Moses Mendelssohn's Jerusalem, which served as a basic text for those who came after him.

These Jews believed that the Torah could also be appreciated as a document subject to the analysis of human reason. They wished to study Torah and secular topics together. They wished to remove from the Torah all those beliefs and *mitzvos* that were embarrassingly non-rational and seemingly primitive: laws of *kashrus*, customs of covering the head, belief in the *Mashiach*, and so on.

Rabbi Sofer was profoundly opposed to these Jewish rationalists. To view the Torah solely through the lens of rationalism reduced the infinite meaning of the Torah to a limited, philosophical text.

But Rabbi Sofer stated that in reality the Torah is infinitely deep and infinitely wise. "The holy Torah is made up of holy Names. That part of the Torah which is hidden has a greater and more eternal holiness than that part of the Torah which is revealed. May we not be blinded, G-d forbid, and believe that the plain meaning of the text of the Bible is the essence of our faith. But those who have gone astray claim that the Bible has nothing but its plain meaning."

As for the *mitzvos*, once one reduced the significance of a *mitzvah* to some rationalistic cause, one paved the way to abandoning the *mitzvah*. Rabbi Sofer stated, "Those who go astray from the Torah try to provide a reason for every commandment of the Torah. As a result, the Torah will be abandoned. They will claim that once a reason is invalidated, the commandment is as well."

If Jews were forbidden to eat pork because in the past there was no way to adequately cook it, then today when it can be properly prepared, why continue to forbid it? "What will happen if we propose reasons for the commandments?" Rabbi Sofer wrote. "The Torah would then become some unimportant text that we could study two or three times and, once we had memorized it, could set aside. If we had any doubt about anything, we could discover the reason for the commandment and know what to do. For example, we could ask, 'Why is pork forbidden?' We could say that it is poisonous. However, what if a certain ingredient was mixed into it so that it was no longer poisonous? But if we instead perform the commandments simply because our King commanded us to, we will admit that we are not able to understand the Bible well enough to make up new laws. Even if the law is contrary to our human reasoning, we will still perform G-d's commandments because the Torah is divine and needs no rationale."

Rabbi Sofer did not deny that there are reasons for the commandments. "G-d forbid that we should claim that the commandments do not have reasons. But those reasons may be complex and unknown to us."

The reasons for the Torah's commandments are not necessarily comprehensible by man. Therefore, any attempt to provide a rationalistic explanation of the commandments was a degradation of Torah. A person who performed *mitzvos* on

171

such a basis was not doing G-d's will. "Even if a person observes the Torah, if he is doing so because of a reason that he thought up, then his act is not acceptable to G-d," taught Rabbi Sofer.

The architects of the new schools that Rabbi Sofer was so much against claimed that children should first learn about the Torah as a universal, rational teaching, together with secular topics. They should learn the plain meaning of the Bible as a text that teaches universal, reasonable laws that teach all mankind how to behave properly. Only afterwards should they be exposed to such things as *Gemara*.

Rabbi Sofer protested, "If children are brought up only learning the plain meaning of the Bible and secular topics, before they ever have a chance to begin studying *Gemara*, which contains the essence of Judaism, they will have already turned against G-d and the Torah." This program of the assimilationists, Rabbi Sofer argued, would lead to the eradication of the unique quality of Judaism and the Jewish people. "One can distinguish between the people of Israel and the gentiles only when the people of Israel completely separate themselves and refrain from studying subjects that they share with us. This includes learning the Bible interpreted according to its plain meaning, for they are equal to us in this."

26

Son-in-Law of Rabbi Akiva Eiger

A CROW SAT UPON A BUDDING TREE BRANCH AND CAWED IN THE wind at the group of people passing beneath him. He lifted his black wings heavily and rose into the cold air, cawing like a messenger running before the group.

Sarah, Rabbi Sofer's wife of twenty-five years, had passed away.

The group of mourners walked slowly to the cemetery, huddled about the six men who carried the pine casket.

Rabbi Sofer delivered a heartfelt eulogy for the woman who had been the partner of his life for a quarter of a century. She had travelled with him, supported him and helped him raise two orphans. Now she was gone. Her kind face would never look at his again. Her presence still filled the house. There was the kitchen, the living room, the dining room—all these rooms were filled with her memory. Now they were bare—bare as the tree branches on a winter's day.

After a few months, people began proposing various matches for Rabbi Sofer. Meir Latersdorf, a very wealthy man, spoke with Rabbi Sofer about his only daughter. If Rabbi Sofer would marry her, she would bring him a dowry of a hundred thousand gulden. Rabbi Sofer considered this proposal seriously.

One day, a letter came to Rabbi Sofer from Rabbi Akiva Eiger, then the rabbi of Markisch-Friedland. Rabbi Sofer and Rabbi Eiger had been on good terms for many years. Rabbi Akiva Eiger wrote that his daughter Seril, a woman with fine qualities, had recently been widowed. Perhaps, wrote Rabbi Akiva Eiger, Rabbi Sofer knew of a good match for her.

Rabbi Sofer did not reply to the letter. Instead, he showed it to his confidante, Rabbi Daniel Prossnitz, *rosh beis din* of Pressburg. "How do you think I should reply?" he asked.

Rabbi Prossnitz was not slow to grasp the initiative. He himself wrote back to Rabbi Akiva Eiger, writing that he knew of a very good match for his daughter: Rabbi Sofer.

Meanwhile, Rabbi Bunim Eiger, Rabbi Akiva Eiger's brother, who was also well-acquainted with Rabbi Sofer, approached Rabbi Sofer directly. He wrote him, "When I heard of the death of your pious wife, I had in mind to write you concerning a possible match, but I didn't see any need to rush things while you were still in mourning . . . But now I would like to commend to you my niece, the widow of the rabbi of Fila, who is without equal.

"I am sure that you intend to marry the daughter of a Torah scholar, brought up in holiness, young, wise, modest and heaven-fearing.

"Thank G-d, she has all these qualities. She is the daughter of a Torah scholar who is the jewel of our generation . . . She has great personal virtues. She is blessed with fear of Heaven and love of Torah, because her previous husband, who headed a *yeshivah*, taught her. She is modest in her actions and very wise. She knows how to act regarding rabbinical matters and how to conduct a household. She is about twenty-four or twenty-five years old . . ."

Once this match was proposed, Rabbi Sofer refused to discuss any other possibilities. He wrote to Rabbi Eiger and asked him a number of questions about the woman. Rabbi Eiger wrote back, praising his daughter at length. However, Rabbi Eiger concluded, there was one matter that stood in the way of the marriage. Rabbi Sofer no doubt wanted to marry the daughter of a Torah scholar. But he, the woman's father, felt that he had not reached this level.

In reply, Rabbi Sofer wrote that he was willing to marry the woman. However, he said, there was one matter that stood in the way of the marriage. Would an outstanding scholar like Rabbi Eiger really want to give his daughter to him?

Soon afterwards, the engagement between the two was made official.

Still, there was another impediment to the marriage of true minds. A number of people resented the idea of these two giants of the generation intermarrying and thus consolidating their authority. They got together and concocted vicious rumors about the woman. "Did you hear what they're saying about Rabbi Akiva's daughter?" they spread the gossip through Pressburg. "She's cold as a fish, short as a dwarf and has hair on her cheeks. She limps and has warts, and she's half-blind, pock-marked, knock-kneed and scruffy."

"What? Rabbi Akiva Eiger's daughter? How can you speak such slander?"

"Slander? *I* speak slander? Oh, please! You don't know how much it hurts me to say these things. But they must be said, and someone has to say them. If we love Rabbi Sofer, how can we keep quiet and allow him to be tricked into such a monstrous marriage?"

Finally, the heads of the community were persuaded to approach Rabbi Sofer and to express their concerns to him. "We have heard these allegations made about Rabbi Eiger's daughter," the head of the delegation said to Rabbi Sofer. "We understand that it is below your dignity to investigate this matter. And we are sure that as a true servant of G-d, you do not put any emphasis on a woman's looks. But as for us, we feel a responsibility to look into the matter."

"I can assure you that I know Rabbi Akiva Eiger and Rabbi Bunim Eiger for many years. They are entirely honorable men. I do not have the slightest doubt in their veracity or their good will. These rumors are ugly falsehoods. Let us ignore them and let them die of inattention, for gossip feeds upon repetition, drinks upon belief and breathes upon spite."

"You are correct, Rabbi Sofer. Yet, is it not possible that there is a grain of truth to these tales? May we not be allowed to do all we can for the sake of our beloved Chief Rabbi?"

Finally, Rabbi Sofer and the leaders agreed to a compromise. Two trustworthy men would be sent to Eisenstadt, Rabbi Eiger's birthplace, where the woman was living with her grandmother. They would meet the woman and speak with her, and would determine for themselves what truth, if any, these rumors possessed.

These two men were soon dispatched to Eisenstadt. As soon as they came to Eisenstadt and met the woman, they realized that the rumors spread about her had been absolutely false. The woman's light shone through these ugly allegations like the light of the full moon when turbid clouds are blown away.

The two men quickly returned to Pressburg and hurried to give their report. They knew that it would not be in keeping with Rabbi Sofer's honor to enter into the details of the matter. Instead, one of the men simply quoted the verse, "This is from G-d; it is wonderful in our eyes." The word "it" in Hebrew also means "she." The verse could be understood, "She is from G-d; she is wonderful in our eyes."

The wedding was quickly arranged so that it could take place before the start of winter, when travelling would be difficult. Rabbi Sofer went to Eisenstadt and there, in *Marcheshvon* of 5573 (1812), he married Seril—a royal marriage between two monarchs of Torah.

People noted that at the time that Rabbi Sofer had married his first wife, his second wife was born. And at the time that Rabbi Sofer's first wife died, the husband of his second wife also died.

Seril brought with her a dowry of 1200 gulden. She had two daughters from her previous marriage. One daughter, Glikl, died as a child. The other, Reidish, grew up and married the well-known Rabbi Yosef Ginz, the son of Rabbi Bunim Eiger.

Altogether, Rabbi Sofer and his wife had ten children: three sons and seven daughters. The oldest son was Rabbi Avraham Shmuel Binyamin Sofer, who eventually took his father's place as Chief Rabbi of Pressburg. Their two other sons were Rabbi Shimon Sofer, Rabbi of Mattersdorf and later of Cracow, and Reb Yuzpa. A fourth son, Yitzchak Leib, died at the age of four.

Their seven daughters were named Hindl, Gitl, Yitl, Simche, Reichl, Reizl and Esther. The first five married outstanding Torah scholars. Reizl and Esther died young after the death of their father.

When their children grew old enough, Seril was very sensitive about her family's fine pedigree and taught them to marry into other families of outstanding Torah background.

Rabbi Sofer supported his household in a dignified manner. He once explained to his son, Avraham Shmuel, that he did so because he felt that, since he was a representative of the Torah, this was necessary to induce people to respect the

Torah. In general, he spent his money freely when he felt that the sanctification of G-d's name was involved.

Unfortunately, he was so busy with his work that he had little time to spend with his children. Nevertheless, he put his trust in G-d that G-d would help those who serve Him to raise their children well.

The couple's first child, born within their first year of marriage, was Hindl.

In 1814, Rabbi Akiva Eiger was offered the post of rabbi of Posen, Germany. Members of his family and friends urged him to accept the post, arguing that it would raise his family's status, including that of Rabbi Sofer. Rabbi Eiger replied, "What does such an illusory honor mean to either me or my son-in-law? To the contrary, I am honored by him, and he has no need of being honored by me." He responded in a similar manner when requested to become rabbi of Vilna, and this letter is reproduced in *Igros Sofrim*.

On the first of *Adar*, 5575 (1815), Seril Sofer was suffering through a hard labor.

"Rabbi Sofer," several of his senior students questioned him, "why don't you pray to G-d to give her an easy delivery?"

"You are right. Ordinarily, I should. But our sages say that when a *tzaddik* is born, another *tzaddik* of a previous generation dies. How can I pray for the good of one person if that will cause harm to another?"

Rabbi Sofer sent a message to his wife, "Do not worry. You will have a son, and he will be not only mine but you will raise him as well."

The boy that was born was named Shmuel Binyamin. His birth began the creation of a dynasty that would preside over a spiritual kingdom transcending the borders of Hungary and the tumultuous period of the nineteenth century.

27

Further Struggles with Reform

THE REFORM MOVEMENT BEGAN TO SPREAD THROUGHOUT GERmany. The movement began its campaign in earnest by advocating changes in the synagogue services.

In 1815, Israel Jacobson moved to Berlin. He had previously been the architect of the Reform position on soldiers' eating legumes on *Pesach*, which Rabbi Sofer and others had so vigorously contested. After having begun a Reform community in Kassel, Jacobson was ready to continue his work in the major city of Germany.

Jacobson opened a house of worship in his own home where prayers and the sermon were delivered in German, and a choir sang in the gentile manner. The *bar-mitzvah* was replaced with the Lutheran-style ceremony of Confirmation. Jacobson's intent was to leave behind the parochial traditions of the Jews and to adopt the more refined customs of the gentiles. This ambition bore fruit, for his own son eventually became a Catholic priest.

The Reform craze to imitate Christianity as much as possible without actually becoming Christian caused embarrassment to a Reform temple in one instance. Members of the Reform movement decided to produce a hymnal similar to the Christian hymnals. In 1816, such a collection, entitled Jewish Hymns, was published. The author of these hymns had simply copied over Lutheran hymns, substituting the phrase, "The Unique One," wherever the name of the founder of Christianity was mentioned in the original. A scandal broke out when someone noticed that, through some oversight, in one instance the original name had been retained.

At any rate, the Reform program of change quickly transformed the synagogue service. The German-language sermon came to be the central element of the Reform service. Sunday became the day of rest.

At first, the non-Jewish authorities were opposed to Reform. In 1816, this temple of Jacobson and another one were ordered closed by the Prussian government.

But in 1819, the Reform movement opened the first official Reform temple, in Hamburg. An organ was played during services, and the prayers were recited in German. The traditional tunes used to read the Torah and *Haftorah* were abandoned. All references to return to the Land of Israel and to the coming of the *Mashiach*, as well as anything having to do with the Beis Hamikdash, were excised.

One of the major Reform leaders in this affair was a man named Eliezer Liebermann. This man issued a pseudo-*halachic* justification of these innovations in a book published in that same year entitled *Nogah Tzedek*. Eventually, Liebermann converted to Catholicism. Aaron Chorin, rabbi of Arad, wrote another polemic tract for Reform called *Or Nogah*. Aaron Chorin really introduced Reform to Hungary, and he was cynically dubbed by the orthodox "Achair," an acronym for Aaron Chorin Rabbiner. (*Achair* was the name given in the Talmud to a sage who departed from the path of righteousness.) Chorin's children eventually converted to Christianity.

The rabbis of Hamburg vigorously contested the legitimacy of this Reform temple and approached the government to help close it down. The government instructed the rabbis of Hamburg to produce a written report giving their view of the controversy, authored by an association of respected rabbis who supported them.

This report was compiled and published under the title, *Eileh Divrei Habris*. It comprised responsa of twenty-two of the most prestigious rabbis of Germany, Hungary, Italy, Prussian Poland, Moravia, Amsterdam and France. Among the contributors were Rabbi Akiva Eiger, Rabbi Mordechai Banet and Rabbi Jacob Lorberbaum of Lissa.

Rabbi Sofer's comments were elicited in a letter by Rabbi Meir Ozers, who wrote him, "Since the [gentile] leaders here [in Hamburg] are intelligent and learned men, they have asked us to bring support to our contentions from our well-known scholars. Therefore, we ask you to please write us expeditiously so that we can show your response to the government and thus annul this temple."

Rabbi Sofer opposed the public nature of such a debate, where important questions relating to Torah were argued between Torah giants and those opposed to Torah, and the ignorant judged who should be victor.

But Rabbi Sofer did pen three of the responsa. Their quality and Rabbi Sofer's stance during this episode made him the outstanding figure in this struggle and brought him to the forefront of communal rabbinic leadership in Europe.

This book was translated into German to give it the widest possible circulation. Even though it was written in a *pilpul* style typical of *halachic* works, it gained wide popularity and was very successful in rebutting the Reform arguments.

When Rabbi Akiva Eiger and Rabbi Mordechai Banet asked Rabbi Sofer to compose a work contesting the claims of *Nogah Tzedek*, Rabbi Sofer replied, "You have asked me to compose a work that challenges *Nogah Tzedek*. I have not hurried to reply, for I know that I am not fit to do this type of public preaching. I do not agree with the idea of publishing such a work. The result will be that they will publish their reply. And those who sit in the coffee houses and cabarets will sit and decide between us.

"Besides, perhaps this evil will be eradicated, so why give it credence for future generations with written records of debates?

"In addition, in every argument that is not for the sake of heaven, evil enters. As you recall, the work *Nogah Tzedek* was composed only after Liebermann was pursued by my father-in-law, as a result of which he joined the Reform movement and composed that book to gain their favor.

"But this is not our way. No stranger shall mix among us, for the holiest sages shall lead this struggle, with their hearts tending only toward the peace of the Torah and service of G-d, and then G-d will be with us."

In general, Rabbi Sofer kept his public remarks to as few as possible. In one letter, he wrote, "I have done three things that I have kept secret even from the rabbis. The reason is that as long as we are at peace amongst ourselves, we can fight G-d's wars and shoot arrows afar to aid our brothers in Hamburg. But if the matter will become known, we will be overwhelmed by controversy even amongst ourselves, for in these times, every vineyard has thorns."

Rabbi Sofer attributed his success to the fact that he always kept his comments free of personal vituperation. "One trait defeated my enemies," he wrote, "and that is that I never fought against an individual. As a result, no individual ever bested me. And I am very distant from seeking this kind of victory."

Elsewhere, he wrote, "I have been very careful not to dispute any particular personality. In my letter I have not mentioned the name of any individual, and I have not fought against any personality. That is not necessary, for truth itself fights falsehood itself."

Rabbi Sofer gained universal praise among the Torah leaders for his role in this episode. Over the course of years, the greatest scholars expressed their great regard for him. Rabbi Mordechai Banet called him "the great and true Torah genius." Rabbi Akiva Eiger called him "the prince of Israel." Rabbi Ephraim Zalman Margolios referred to him as "the head of the exile." Rabbi Moshe Mintz called him "the great one of the generation." Rabbi Moshe Teitelbaum called him "the wonder of the generation, the holy lamp."

The intent of the Reform program was to become refined and civilized like the gentiles. In the same year that the Reform movement fought to establish its Temple, the gentile world exploded in violent anti-Jewish riots. Across the cities of Germany, including Hamburg, pogroms broke out in the summer of 1819. These pogroms were not merely the spontaneous outpouring of hatred of the ignorant. The refined and civilized professors of Germany themselves preached hatred of the Jew.

Across Germany, the ancient anti-Semitic slogan of the Crusades was revived by the learned academics: Hierosolyma est perdita—Jerusalem is lost. Mobs shouted the acronym of this slogan—hep—as they ransacked Jewish neighborhoods. "Hep, hep, Jude verrecke—Hep, hep, perish, Jew!" (This is the source of the seemingly innocuous phrase, "Hip, hip, hooray!")

Benighted zealots of Reform, knights of assimilation bowed before the fair prince of gentile culture and galloped off to joust against the Orthodox Jews whom they despised! They did not suspect that when the horse was wheeled around the prince would string his bow and drive a shaft through their exposed back.

But not all the slings and arrows could quench the ardor of the Reformers. If they were attacked again and still persecuted, there could be only one reason: they were still too Jewish. There could be only one response: to assimilate more. And so by 1823, many of the Jewish population of Berlin had converted to Christianity. But the Reform theoreticians were baffled, for this gift of self-sacrifice to the idol of assimilation still did not appease its mighty wrath. And so the demon of Orthodoxy was again invoked as the cause of the gentiles' enmity.

And meanwhile in Hungary, the Reform movement encountered fierce opposition from the Orthodox community unlike anything it had encountered anywhere else. This was directly due to the influence of Rabbi Sofer.

28

Life in Pressburg

IT IS TOLD THAT ON THE EVE OF *YOM KIPPUR* OF 5580 (1820), RABBI
Moshe Teitelbaum, the great *Chassidic* leader and author of
Yismach Moshe, looked up to see an apparition of a handsome, dark-bearded Jew standing silently before him. Although he had never met Rabbi Sofer, Rabbi Teitelbaum
realized it was he. But what did he want? The vision gave no
hint.

Still, Rabbi Teitelbaum realized that he must desire something, and on *Yom Kippur*, he prayed for the good of Rabbi
Sofer in a general way.

Immediately after *Yom Kippur*, Rabbi Teitelbaum summoned a student of Rabbi Sofer who was living in his area, and
asked him, "Please tell me what Rabbi Sofer looks like."

"He has dark brown hair, a medium-length, neatly-combed
beard, his nose is aquiline and flares a little, his left eye has just

a bit of a cast, and he wears a soft, fur hat."

Rabbi Teitelbaum was now sure that it was Rabbi Sofer who had come to him. But why?

The next day, someone brought a letter to Rabbi Teitelbaum. Rabbi Teitelbaum opened the envelope and saw that it came from Rabbi Sofer.

"When did you receive this letter?" he asked the man.

"I got it the day before *Yom Kippur*. But since I knew how busy you are, I didn't want to disturb you."

Rabbi Teitelbaum grew very upset at the man. He turned his attention to the letter. Rabbi Sofer wrote that all his children were deathly ill, and he begged Rabbi Teitelbaum to pray for their health.

Rabbi Teitelbaum realized that since he hadn't read the letter, Rabbi Sofer's spirit had come in person to seek his aid.

Rabbi Sofer himself prayed at great length for the recovery of his children. At one point, Eliyahu Hanavi himself came to Rabbi Sofer and told him what would happen to his children. They would all recover—except for one. His youngest child was not slated for life in this world. From that point on, Rabbi Sofer grew somber.

At that time, he gave his eldest son, Shmuel Binyamin, the additional name of Avraham. Once, Rabbi Sofer returned from his prayers and told those around him, "I have been granted an extension of fifty years." His mysterious words were clarified when this son lived for exactly fifty more years. However, he was throughout his life plagued by ill health.

Rabbi Sofer ruled his emotions like a governor rules a city. During the terrible period when all his children were ill, he never missed a day of his regular study schedule.

Once, during this time, he returned to his house after pouring out his heart in prayer, and he composed a very long and complex letter regarding a very serious matter involving the laws of marriage.

As he sat writing the letter, one of his students, Rabbi
Fishel Sofer, came into the room.

"Rabbi Sofer!" he exclaimed. "How can you sit here so
calmly and write such a letter, which requires a calm and clear
head, when you are in the middle of such sorrow?"

Rabbi Sofer looked up at his student. "There is a time for
prayer," he said, "and a time for Torah. Now is the time for
Torah." And he calmly leaned over and resumed his writing.

Sukkos came, and Rabbi Sofer's children still lay deathly
ill. One day, the tragedy that Eliyahu Hanavi had predicted
struck. Rabbi Sofer's four-year-old son's soul escaped the
prison of his body. But Rabbi Sofer ruled over himself. Today
was *Sukkos*—the holiday of joy. His principal responsibility
was to serve G-d, and this was the time of serving G-d through
joy. Later, he would mourn.

One day on *Sukkos*, Rabbi Sofer came home to find his
wife Seril weeping.

"Do not weep," he told her. "It is a holiday, and we are
forbidden to mourn today."

Seril dried her tears and did not cry for the remainder of
the holiday.

Still, Rabbi Sofer's other children lay sick. As Rabbi Sofer
sat at the table in the *Sukkah* with his family, he suddenly said,
"I hear people saying *Tehillim*. Perhaps they are reciting
Tehillim in the synagogue."

Someone went out to see. He came back, shaking his head.
"The synagogue is empty."

"If *Tehillim* isn't being said below," Rabbi Sofer said,
"then is it being said above."

Little by little, all his other children recovered from their
illness.

As he grew up into young adulthood, Avraham Shmuel
Binyamin studied with great perseverance. But he hid his
diligence from his father to such a degree that Rabbi Sofer

came to suspect the boy of laziness. At night, Avraham Shmuel would go to bed and feign sleep until he heard his father fall asleep. Only then would he steal out of bed and learn throughout the night. His father was led to believe that the boy slept for very long.

Although he wrote original Torah thoughts, he kept these a secret from his father as well. But his application and brilliance could not be forever concealed. By the age of seventeen, he was already answering *halachic* questions that were being mailed to him.

Rabbi Sofer's days of travel were over. He remained in Pressburg for the rest of his life, establishing Torah learning and *mitzvah* observance as a way of life for Jews for generations to come. Although he appeared to be a public man, involved in communal and political affairs, he was essentially a man of Torah, and his life revolved about the day-to-day process of serving G-d via the Torah.

He once said that since he had reached the age of ten, he had never walked a distance of ten cubits (about fifteen feet) without learning Torah, and that no day had ever passed without his creating novel Torah thoughts.

Another time, Rabbi Sofer told his son, Avraham Shmuel Binyamin, that from the moment that he had reached a level of maturity, a strange thought had never entered his prayer. Also, a desire for honor had never entered his heart when he taught, with one exception: when he became rabbi of Dressnitz, in his first talk to the community, he wanted to prove how expert he was. But even then, his desire that the people respect him was only so that they would heed him.

Earlier, Rabbi Sofer's day-to-day and *Shabbos* customs were noted. He also had specific customs regarding the holidays.

Rabbi Sofer fasted on the eve of *Rosh Hashanah*. When he returned home from the synagogue, he was accompanied by the important members of the community, headed by the *dayan*. They all wished him a good year, and he then gave a talk based on the verse, "In order that your days may be increased," including the *Sifri's* commentary on this verse. Then he quoted the verse, "And those who love Him are like the sun coming out in its strength," and he blessed all the members of the community.

At the *Rosh Hashanah* meal, all the types of food mentioned in the *Shulchan Aruch* as auspicious for the coming year were brought to the table.

Besides these vegetables and the salad he ate for *marror* on *Pesach*, Rabbi Sofer never ate any other leafy vegetables or any vegetables that need to be checked for bugs. Similarly, unless he had the opportunity to make a *shehechiyanu* blessing on a new fruit in season, he did not eat fruits that needed checking.

On the second night of *Rosh Hashanah*, Rabbi Daniel Prossnitz sent Rabbi Sofer a basket of fruits that were in season, especially selected by the farmer.

For *Tashlich*, Rabbi Sofer went to the garden behind his house, from which he could see the Danube River. He recited the verses, "Who is a god like You?" three times, and added nothing else. Afterwards, he sat in the garden gazebo with his family and Torah scholars, and he was brought fruits to eat.

Although Rabbi Sofer prayed throughout the year in the *beis midrash* among his students and other Torah scholars, on the eve of holidays and during the days of *Selichos*, he prayed in the large synagogue. He did this for the honor of the community, even though he found it difficult to tolerate the cantor's elaborate style, accompanied by a choir. In one letter, Rabbi Sofer wrote bitingly, "A cantor does not fulfill the *halachic* requirements even on the Days of Awe. When he puts his hand on his chin and cries out like a crow, will G-d hear such a cry?"

189

On the eve of holidays, after the prayers, he would bless his sons in the synagogue, and he would then interpret a verse relating to the holiday.

Rabbi Sofer also went to the large synagogue every *Shabbos* and holiday after he had finished *Mussaf*. He would arrive before the large synagogue had begun the reading of the Torah, and he would remain there until *Mussaf* was over.

During the recital of *Selichos*, Rabbi Sofer said the entire book of *Tehillim*. Then he remained a long while in the synagogue after *Selichos* were over. It is said that during that time, he went through the entire six orders of the *Mishnah* together with the commentary, *Eitz Chaim* of Rabbi Chagiz, as well as quickly reviewing the entire Talmud, Jerusalem Talmud, *Sifra*, *Sifrei* and *Tosefta*.

During these days, he learned the laws of penitence in the *Rambam* with his students before noon.

On his birthday, the seventh of *Tishrei*, Rabbi Sofer completed the *Chumash* with his students and gave each student four coins with which to buy dairy pastries. He kept this custom even for those students who fasted Mondays and Thursdays.

On the eve of *Yom Kippur*, Rabbi Sofer's *kapparos* chicken was slaughtered at dawn before he went to *Selichos*, in accordance with the opinion of the Ari. However, Rabbi Sofer admonished others not to emulate him in this. This would burden the slaughterers and force them to slaughter many birds in a short period of time, leading to possible *halachic* problems. He said that unless one knows exactly when dawn is, it makes no difference when one slaughters the bird within the period from the *Tzom Gedaliah* to the eve of *Yom Kippur*.

After *Shacharis*, Rabbi Sofer gathered a group of older men and recited the ceremony of absolution of vows before them. He then went into another room and came out in his stocking feet to accept rebuke, but the others excused him from having to do so.

He went to the *mikveh* before midday, and then ate. He recited *Minchah* in the synagogue and then returned home, accompanied by the leaders and scholars of the city. He blessed each person individually and then ate the last meal before *Yom Kippur*. Then his children and other family members came to him. He blessed them with tears in his eyes, and asked them to pray for him. Then he again went to the *mikveh*.

Before *Kol Nidrei*, Rabbi Sofer gave a talk on the holiness of the day. After the service was over, he went through the first book of *Tehillim* with the congregation. Then he told the people to recite the *Kesser Malchus* of the Radbaz (rather than of Ben Gabirol).

Rabbi Sofer returned joyously to his house carrying a bundle of spices. His students were waiting for him, and he wished them a good holiday. He learned with them the order of the *Yom Kippur* service in the Beis Hamikdash until "the appearance of the *kohein*." Then he propounded a question in the laws of penitence that he had dealt with on *Shabbos Shuvah*. Afterwards, he learned from wherever he was up to in the Talmud.

This lasted until about one in the morning. When Rabbi Sofer's students saw that he was growing drowsy, they took their leave. As they left, Rabbi Sofer told them, "Go, my sons, and pray for me today." With these words, Rabbi Sofer's eyes filled with tears, and he and his students cried together. Then Rabbi Sofer's students asked him to bless them and he did so, one by one, to which they replied, "*Amein*, and so may it be for you." If anyone did not reply in this way, Rabbi Sofer would admonish him. That night, he did not sleep in bed.

During *Shacharis*, other people came to receive his blessing.

The *Kohanim* blessed the people even at *Shacharis*.

Rabbi Sofer stood on his feet throughout the entire day, even in his old age.

He finished the final blessing of *Shmoneh Esrei* with the same words as those said during the rest of the year: "He Who blesses His people with peace." He said that in Moravia, there had been two camps. One said "He Who blesses with peace," and the other said, "He Who makes peace," and they fought constantly about whether to make peace or bless peace.

Although the leaders of the community regularly asked Rabbi Sofer to lead the prayers for *Ne'ilah*, as is customary for the town rabbi, he never did so.

Immediately after *Yom Kippur*, Rabbi Sofer went to see if his *sukkah* was properly covered. He used *lulavim* as the covering.

On the eve of holidays, fathers brought their sons to Rabbi Sofer for a blessing.

Every holiday, Rabbi Sofer bought an animal. He slaughtered this animal and separated the gifts for the *kohanim* that had been brought during the time of the Beis Hamikdash.

For *Sukkos*, Rabbi Sofer always went out of his way to buy a Genoese *esrog*, saying that those *esrogim* were the most kosher. He also bought a second, especially beautiful *esrog*. Every day, he would wave the *lulav* in his *sukkah* in a fiery manner, omitting the new prayers that people had started adding before doing the *mitzvah*.

Rabbi Sofer ate in the *sukkah* together with all his sons, daughters, sons-in-law and daughters-in-law throughout *Sukkos*. After each meal, he handed out nuts and sweetmeats. However, except for the first night of *Sukkos*, he did not tell the women to remain in the *sukkah* for the entire meal. He instructed women not to make a blessing on sitting in a *sukkah*.

Rabbi Sofer ate, slept, learned and prayed *Minchah* and

Maariv in the *sukkah* and remained there almost constantly during the holiday. He ate nothing outside the *sukkah*. During *Sukkos*, Rabbi Sofer held the *lulav* in his hand while praying. He put on *tefillin* and wrote his Torah thoughts during *Chol Hamoed*.

On the eve of *Hoshanna Rabbah*, Rabbi Sofer stayed up in the *sukkah* with his colleagues and students saying the *tikkun* (with several deletions) until about two in the morning, when he went to sleep.

His *Hoshanna Rabbah aravah* had seventeen branches.

On the night of *Shemini Atzeres*, Rabbi Sofer did not sleep in the *sukkah*. After the day meal, he left the *sukkah*. He was brought fruits, which he ate.

After *Minchah*, Rabbi Sofer gave a talk to the Torah scholars and students. Then he prayed *Maariv* and made *hakafos*. Three Torah scrolls were brought to the *bimah*. *Al Hakol* was sung, and Rabbi Fishel Sofer sang four songs that Rabbi Sofer had composed for *Simchas Torah*. Then they sang *Ein Keilokeinu* in both Hebrew and Yiddish, and then some *Tehillim* and *Adon Olam*.

Rabbi Sofer's colleagues and students accompanied him home and brought him delicacies. He gave out wine and cake, and each student sang a song. These songs were also sung on the eve of the first night of *Purim* after breaking the fast. This celebration came to an end shortly before midnight.

In the morning, Rabbi Sofer prayed at dawn, and the *kohanim* blessed the people during *Shacharis*. Rabbi Sofer stood directly before the *kohanim*.

Rabbi Sofer was always the *Chassan Torah*, and he would always pledge eighteen liters of oil for the lamps.

Afterwards, he went to the large synagogue and celebrated the *hakafos* there as well. There, he was also called third to the Torah and again as *Chassan Torah*.

On both *Simchas Torah* and *Purim*, he said *Minchah*

before eating the day meal.

Rabbi Sofer admonished people to be especially careful about learning Torah on *Chanukah*. During this time, G-d had taught Moshe Rabbeinu great secrets of Torah, but people tended to spend this time playing games.

On *Motzei Shabbos*, Rabbi Sofer made *Havdalah* before lighting the *Chanukah* candles, saying that the miracle of *Chanukah* is not mentioned in the *Mishnah*. He said that the reason for this was that Rabbi Yehudah Hanasi, author of the *Mishnah*, was descended from King David, and the miracle of *Chanukah* was carried out by the family of the *Chashmonaim*, who, although not of King David's offspring, took power. This bothered Rabbi Yehudah Hanasi, and when he wrote the *Mishnah* by Divine inspiration, he skipped over this miracle.

On *Tu b'Shevat*, Rabbi Sofer ate many fruits.

After the meal following the Fast of Esther, Rabbi Sofer was joined by Torah scholars and his students, and they sang all the songs of *Simchas Torah*, and in addition the song *Orah Lemordechai*.

On *Purim*, Rabbi Sofer supported the custom of banging when Haman's name was mentioned.

Immediately upon returning home from prayers in the morning, he sent out *mishloach manos* to other Torah scholars, without waiting to be sent *mishloach manos* first.

Frankfurt-am-Main, the city of his birth, celebrated a *Purim* for its own miracle on the twentieth of *Adar I*. Rabbi Sofer celebrated this as well. But in order to have no doubts about the propriety of doing so, he made sure to celebrate a *siyum* that day.

On the night of *Pesach*, Rabbi Sofer did not recite *Hallel*.

At the Seder, Rabbi Sofer set aside for his wife a chair on which it was comfortable to lean. He was not strict about eating the *afikomen* before midnight, but continued the seder until one or two o'clock in the morning. He dedicated this time to the small boys and girls. He translated the *Haggadah* for them word for word and explained it to them, and did not address the adults with any talk. After the first cup of wine, he handed nuts out to the children, beginning with the youngest.

During the recital of the ten plagues, Rabbi Sofer poured wine out of his cup by using his finger, and not by tipping over the cup.

For *marror*, Rabbi Sofer used salad that had been checked by *yeshivah* students with a magnifying glass.

When the *seder* was completed, Rabbi Sofer asked the women to go to sleep, with the exception of the young girls. He then sang a number of songs appended to the *Haggadah*. He translated some of the songs into Yiddish for the girls. He did this to make sure that they would stay up until the end of the seder.

Then he learned the Song of Songs with his students, with Rashi's commentary. When his students saw that he was growing drowsy, they left, and he slept till dawn on the couch. By six o'clock, he was in the *beis midrash* ready for the morning prayers.

After the seder, Rabbi Sofer drank coffee. On the second day of *Pesach*, he ate a dried tongue, in memory of the hanging of Haman on that day. On the seventh of *Pesach*, Rabbi Sofer ate the tongue of an animal with a sharp sauce, possibly in memory of the three tongues that the angels who visited Abraham ate on *Pesach*.

On *Shavuos* night, Rabbi Sofer recited the entire *Tikkun* together with his students.

In the morning, one student who had slept made all the morning blessings for everyone. Then, after sleeping in the morning, everyone made the blessings for himself.

Until he grew old, Rabbi Sofer used to fast in the period between the seventeenth of *Tammuz* and *Tishah b'Av*.

On *Tishah b'Av*, Rabbi Sofer went to his room in the

afternoon until *Minchah*, and no one knew what he did there.

These were Rabbi Sofer's customs throughout the year.

One day, a stranger was greeted with an unusual reception. Rabbi Sofer took him into his private room and remained secreted with him for a long time. When the man parted at last, Rabbi Sofer gave him some money and a letter of support.

"What is this? This is not Rabbi Sofer's way. What special merit did this stranger have?" The questions circled through the *beis midrash*.

One of the students cautiously asked Rabbi Sofer these questions. Rabbi Sofer replied, "The man who just left here caused me a great deal of worry for many years. I have told you that when I was Rabbi Nassan Adler's student, he had a number of people who persecuted him. Once, when I asked Rabbi Adler if it was just that he should suffer while they prosper, he told me that eventually every single one of them would come to me seeking assistance.

"And so it happened over the years that they all came, with the exception of this man. For all these years I was very worried that Rabbi Adler's words might not come completely true. But now that this man came to me seeking my aid, I see Rabbi Adler's great power, and the truth of our sages' warning, 'Be wary of the coal of Torah sages, for their bite is the bite of a snake and their sting is the sting of a scorpion.'"

As the trouble-makers of the previous generation thinned out, their ranks were filled with alacrity by the eager practitioners of the art. But their enthusiasm kindled a like ardor for battle in the camp of their adversary, and a renewed commitment to Orthodoxy.

29

Strengthening Orthodoxy

IN THE WAKE OF THE ECONOMIC CHAOS CAUSED BY THE WARS against Napoleon and the resulting political instability, the economic status of Austrian and Hungarian Jews declined precipitously. The community of Pressburg was compelled to inform Rabbi Sofer that it could not uphold its commitment to support the *yeshivah* that he had so laboriously fostered.

At the same time, as a result of the spreading Reform movement, the community of Fuerth, Germany was inspired to increase its level of commitment to Torah. In 5580 (1820), when the rabbi of Fuerth, Rabbi Meshullam Zalman (author of *Bigdei Kehunah*) passed away, the community invited Rabbi Sofer to accept the position of chief rabbi.

Rabbi Sofer replied, "Here in Pressburg, I am in a community of kosher and G-d-fearing people, among whom are outstanding Torah scholars . . . My only desire is to share with others of the little amount of Torah knowledge that G-d has bestowed upon me. I teach about 250 students . . . However, they are very poor."

Rabbi Sofer went on to explain that he would be willing to move if the community of Fuerth would "please write me explicitly, telling how my students would be supported, and if it is your desire to support a *yeshivah* both liberally and legally."

The rumor spiralled with rapidity through Pressburg that Rabbi Sofer was considering relocating to Germany. The community leaders convened an emergency session during which they petitioned Rabbi Sofer not to leave. But Rabbi Sofer was implacable.

Rabbi Hirsch Yaffe rose and declared, "Rabbi Sofer, it is manifest that when you depart for Fuerth, you will propagate Torah to all of Germany. But to the extent that you foster Fuerth and all Germany in consequence, so will Pressburg plummet, and all Hungary in its aftermath. How can you leave us on such a basis?"

This argument shattered Rabbi Sofer's plans, and he acquiesced to the desire of the community leaders.

There had been no *yeshivah* as large and important as that of Rabbi Sofer since the times of the *geonim*. The *yeshivah* always housed at least several hundred students, many of them outstanding Torah scholars.

With Rabbi Sofer's active help, his students became rabbis throughout Hungary. These students were as dedicated and uncompromising as Rabbi Sofer in their defense of traditional Judaism. Now when a community wanted to choose a rabbi, it would be faced with the choice between a follower of Rabbi Sofer and a follower of the Reform movement. There was increasingly little room for an intermediary position.

In response to the challenge of the growing Reform movement, the Orthodox rabbi was accorded more authority than he had wielded in previous years. His authority unified the community and gave it strength. This was a centralization of power actively supported by Rabbi Sofer.

Rabbi Sofer believed that every town had an obligation to appoint a rabbi and not to leave the post unfilled for any appreciable time. In addition, Rabbi Sofer held that the community was obligated to pay the rabbi an adequate salary. Rabbi Sofer stated his opinion that a rabbi had no reason to be ashamed of accepting a salary for his work. It was appropriate for him to accept money in exchange for leading a community.

Rabbi Sofer also supported the trend toward giving a community rabbi lifetime tenure. He stated that even though a typical contract only gave a chief rabbi three years' tenure, this was merely a formal statement that did not give the community the right to dismiss him.

Finally, in his later years, Rabbi Sofer ruled that a rabbi had the right to bequeath his position to his son (as he himself eventually did).

These positions of Rabbi Sofer served to strengthen the position of the traditional, Orthodox rabbinate, and erected a formidable defense against Reform strategies.

Baron Rothschild of Vienna wished to petition Hungary's government to appoint Rabbi Sofer as Chief Rabbi of all Hungary and to allow only him to appoint and dismiss rabbis.

Baron Rothschild approached Rabbi Sofer with this proposal, but Rabbi Sofer dismissed it. "With G-d's help, I would use such a post well," he said. "But who knows who would come after me? Someone else might make conditions worse."

In the spring of 1820, members of the Reform movement opened an elementary school in Pressburg that enrolled ten students from observant families. The head of the community, Avraham Hirsch Lemberger, and several others responded by sitting in mourning for a week.

But Rabbi Sofer's reaction was swift and more effective. He opened a trade school the same year. This was the first school of its kind to operate in Hungary. Now parents who were concerned that their children learn a practical craft could send their children to a fully Orthodox school. In Rabbi Sofer's school, Torah, writing, reading, languages and vocational skills were taught by religious instructors. But in general, Rabbi Sofer was firmly opposed to the learning of general studies.

The Reform attack on traditional values had signalled the beginning of a siege on Torah, and Rabbi Sofer was the commanding officer of the forces of Torah. In effect he declared martial law. Every issue became sharply politicized and polarized. The Reform movement manipulated and exploited all changes and all innovations as tools by the Reform movement to drive a wedge into the Orthodox camp. Rabbi Sofer responded with equal firmness. All change and all innovation was henceforth suspect and forbidden.

A favorite slogan of Rabbi Sofer was, "*Chadash assur min Hatorah*: Whatever is new is forbidden by the Torah."

Rabbi Sofer fought tenaciously in defense of even the slightest of Jewish customs. He wrote, "I am sure that you will not mock any Jewish customs whose reasons we no longer know, because they are rooted in a well of living waters. It is my custom to say that whoever is skeptical about such customs must be investigated. When a person's Torah is his way of life, when he is wrapped in fear of G-d and he is not involved in gentile matters, he will not make an error. But a person who mixes books of logic with words of Torah transgresses the prohibition against plowing with an ox and a donkey together. If such a person is a leader of the Jews, it is as though he is plowing with two different species."

Every *Shavuos*, the synagogue was decorated with fragrant grasses and trees, and a garland of branches and herbs was arched over Rabbi Sofer's seat. One year, one of the *gabbaim*, who objected to this custom, didn't allow the branches to be brought into the synagogue. When Rabbi Sofer came to the synagogue and saw that the custom had been discontinued, he grew angry at the *gabbai*. Within a year, the man died.

The reason Rabbi Sofer was so strict about keeping Jewish customs was that they are a fence to the essence of Torah. Whoever wanted to change a custom was suspect of possibly wanting to weaken the Torah itself.

When the first Reform temple was built in Vienna, the heads of the city turned to Rabbi Sofer and Rabbi Mordechai Banet for official permission to alter a few customs regarding the shape of the building and the like.

Neither rabbi responded. When Rabbi Banet was asked about this, he replied, "If I knew that these people really only wanted to change these few customs, I would try to find some reason to permit them, even though customs are very important. This would be like a doctor cutting off a limb to save the body. In order to keep these people from straying further, I would give them what they wanted.

"But I am aware that this is only the beginning. These people's intent is to undermine everything. But because they are afraid of those who are loyal to the Torah, they begin in this manner. I will certainly not help such people. If I do, they will claim that pious people support them. And I have no doubt that Rabbi Sofer refused to respond for the same reason."

Rabbi Sofer was not rigid in his approach. One *Simchas Torah*, a Polish Jew visiting Pressburg started singing a chapter of *Tehillim* in German translation. In horror and indignation, Rabbi Sofer's students silenced the man. Wasn't Rabbi Sofer the great fighter against the translation of the Torah into German? How dare this man come into Rabbi Sofer's own synagogue and do such a thing?

But Rabbi Sofer interrupted, "My students, you have done wrong. Allow me, if you please, to take care of my own business." He turned to the man. "Are you singing *Tehillim* to the translation of Moses Mendelssohn?"

"No," replied the man.

"In that case, I would ask you to continue from where you left off," Rabbi Sofer said. Later, to stress his support of this visitor, Rabbi Sofer invited him to his house.

Rabbi Sofer's ability to judge individual cases on their own merits also contributed to his fame as a writer of *halachic* letters—*teshuvos*.

As a general rule, Rabbi Sofer would make his *halachic* decisions only on the basis of the Talmud, the Jerusalem Talmud and the *midrashim*. He followed the custom of his two rabbis, Rabbi Adler and Rabbi Horowitz, of never allowing *Kabbalistic* teachings to influence his *halachic* decisions. "Whoever mixes words of *Kabbalah* with *Halachah*," he wrote, "is guilty of the sin of sowing *kilayim*, even though you may grow wheat and you may grow vines, the Torah forbids mixing the two!"

Letters came to Rabbi Sofer during his midday meal and he would ask one of his sons to read them to him.

The letters opened with flowery salutations, praising Rabbi Sofer as the "leader of the generation" and the "teacher of Israel." When Rabbi Sofer would hear these titles, he would groan. Upon hearing his father's reaction, Rabbi Sofer's son Shimon would smile. It seemed to him that his father was, in his modesty, denying the truth of these epithets.

One day, when Rabbi Sofer became aware of his son's attitude, he said to him, "'I do not groan because I think that I am not what these letters call me. Rather, I am upset about what kind of generation this is that a person like me should be a leader."

Rabbi Sofer wrote at length, without hesitation. He almost

never had to rewrite anything. In addition, he used to write his letters swiftly. Once his son, Avraham Shmuel Binyamin, asked him, "'Father, where do you get the self-confidence to send *halachic* replies out so quickly, even on the most serious issues? Aren't you afraid that in your haste you might make a mistake?"

Rabbi Sofer replied, "'My son, I am well aware that it is no small matter to make a *halachic* decision, and that *halachah* demands clarity. But you must be aware that in every generation, G-d has appointed a man to be a leader of the congregation, to guide the people and answer their questions. Since most people turn to me when they have questions in *halachah*, it appears that I have the approval of Heaven. I thank G-d that I have learned sufficiently and that my intent is for the sake of Heaven alone.

"'As a result, I do not suspect G-d of causing me to fail. I am assured that He will agree to my decisions.

"At times, it may even be that my proof is questionable. Nevertheless, my final decision is true.'"

Once, Rabbi Meir Asch sent Rabbi Sofer a difficult question. Rabbi Meir Asch was very close to Rabbi Sofer and when they were together, he would discuss all his questions in learning with Rabbi Sofer, as well as personal issues. After completing his meal, Rabbi Sofer penned a reply and, before mailing it, showed it to Avraham Shmuel Binyamin. In this way, he was providing his son with an apprenticeship in *halachic* decisions.

A few days later, a second letter arrived from Rabbi Meir Asch with a number of questions regarding some of the statements that Rabbi Sofer had made.

Again, Rabbi Sofer penned a quick reply, showing the letter to his son before he mailed it out.

Avraham Shmuel Binyamin asked his father, "Father, I know how highly you value Rabbi Meir Asch. Yet you wrote to him so quickly, apparently without deeply considering what you were saying. But now that he has written back and questioned some of your points, you seem upset."

"My son," Rabbi Sofer answered, "my *halachic* decision was correct. And so what does it matter to me if some proof that I brought was not exact? A Torah scholar like him should understand that."

Some time later, Rabbi Meir Asch wrote again, apologizing profusely. He clarified that he had not questioned Rabbi Sofer's decision at all, but had only wanted to clear up a point about one of the proofs.

Another time, Rabbi Yosef Ginz, stepson-in-law of Rabbi Sofer, was learning with another Torah scholar in Rabbi Sofer's house. They came to a difficult question and asked him to clarify it for them.

Rabbi Sofer answered the question, but the two scholars fell into a heated debate with him. Finally, they seemed to have bested him, and they left his room.

A short while later, Rabbi Sofer called them back and told them, "An old ignoramus knows more than young scholars. I know that the law is what I said it is, even though for the moment I couldn't bring a proof. But since then, I've thought it over and I can now prove my point."

Although Rabbi Sofer's students often pressed him to publish his responsa, he refused to do so, just as Rabbi Adler had not published any of his own writings.

Once, when someone asked to see a copy of something Rabbi Sofer had written, he replied, "You have heard that I wrote a composition, and you have requested that I send it to you.

"I have never considered doing such a thing. It never occurred to me that I should send out what I have written. People who are greater than or on my level do not need to see what I have written. And as for that small minority of people that is less-accomplished than I, why should I work so hard for the sake of a small minority?

"Even if the majority of people need me, I don't see why I am required to publish material while I am still alive. While G-d gives me strength, I am ready to learn with whoever comes to listen. With G-d's help, I will reply to all questions sent to me, whether in *halachah* or *Aggadah*. In addition, anyone who wants can come to my house and read my writings or copy them as he wishes. This was how things were done in the generations before the invention of printing, and I am not obligated to do any more."

Rabbi Sofer's ability to write authoritative *teshuvos* was facilitated by his extraordinary memory. This memory was the result of his hard work on himself. When a person sees something remarkable, it sticks in his mind. Similarly, every word that Rabbi Sofer learned was so remarkable to him that he didn't forget it.

Rabbi Sofer relied not only on his intellect but also on an inspired intuition to make his *halachic* decisions. Once, a woman was seeking permission to remarry after the disappearance of her husband. Many Torah authorities had already given their approval. But when the case came before Rabbi Sofer, he stated, "My heart tells me that this woman's husband is still alive." The woman didn't remarry and after a short while, her husband returned to her.

But Rabbi Sofer no longer continued to write poetry, as he had done in Dressnitz. Once he explained, "When I was younger, I would take stock of myself when the holidays came. I would see that I had achieved as much as I could possibly expect of myself. I would be filled with joy. Then a spirit of song would flow through me, and I would write down my poetry.

"But here in Pressburg, I have so many obligations that I do not have enough time to adequately develop my spiritual self.

As a result, I have not been inspired to write poetry."

In this way, Rabbi Sofer expressed the crucial connection between spiritual greatness and the creative, poetic spirit.

30

The Mystic

THE PEAL OF TRUMPETS RENT THE AIR, SIGNALLING THE WEDDING OF Rabbi Sofer's sister's son, Rabbi Shmuel Strauss, who had grown up in his house. Soon afterwards, Rabbi Sofer was again learning in the *beis midrash*.

Rabbi Sofer's *beis midrash* was a place of miracles. Rabbi Sofer once wrote a letter to Rabbi Ephraim Zalman Margolios, whom he never met but with whom he felt extremely close. Rabbi Sofer wrote, "We have learned that in the crowded Beis Hamikdash, the people were able to prostrate themselves as a result of a miracle that was given to them as a reward for coming to the Beis Hamikdash. The Tashbatz writes that in his time as well, such a miracle occurred in a synagogue in Jerusalem on *Shavuos*. And G-d is my witness that I have seen this outside the Land of Israel. But because of those people who mock such matters, I cannot be more explicit."

One day, when Shimon, Rabbi Sofer's son, was still a boy, a friend came to visit him at his home. They began speaking about his father's greatness.

"Your father is visited by Eliyahu Hanavi!"

"He is?"

"I know it for sure!"

"No, you're making it up!"

Shimon's friend opened the door. "Go on, ask him yourself!" he said, and shoved Shimon into the other room.

Shimon staggered across the threshold.

"Yes?" Rabbi Sofer looked up from his *Gemara*. "What is it, Shimon?"

"Uh, well . . ."

"What do you want?"

Reluctantly, Shimon repeated to his father the argument that he and his friend had been having.

Rabbi Sofer looked at him and said, "Your friend is right. But you should know that even when Eliyahu does appear to a person, he can do so on many different levels."

Another time, Rabbi Sofer sat learning with his son, Rabbi Avraham Shmuel Binyamin, and two other students. Suddenly, a stranger entered the room. Rabbi Sofer stood up. "Welcome," he said. He turned to the others. "Wait here." Rabbi Sofer and the other man went into a nearby room and remained there for a while.

When Rabbi Sofer returned, he asked, "Did any of you greet that man?"

"I did," said Rabbi Sofer's son and one of the students. But the third student, who was the oldest, admitted that he hadn't.

"Fortunate is he who has greeted Eliyahu Hanavi," Rabbi Sofer exclaimed, "and fortunate is he who has been greeted in turn."

Although Rabbi Sofer had vast erudition in *Kabbalah* and mysticism, he kept his involvement in this area hidden. In later years, his colleague Rabbi Daniel Prossnitz reported that Rabbi Sofer had once told him, "Among the great leaders of our generation, I have found only one person who has as much authority as I in *Kabbalah*." Rabbi Prossnitz added, "Everyone knows that Rabbi Sofer was unique in his generation in his mastery of the revealed aspects of the Torah. But I will tell you what you do not know: that he was even greater in his knowledge of *Kabbalah*."

Although Rabbi Prossnitz was Rabbi Sofer's elder, he accepted Rabbi Sofer as his mentor and learned *Kabbalah* from him.

Even though Rabbi Sofer was secretive about his involvement in *Kabbalah*, preferring to "walk humbly with G-d," many times he was asked to use his knowledge of *Kabbalah* and holy names of G-d to help people who were suffering. In his holiness and modesty, Rabbi Sofer usually turned down such requests, for he opposed making use of *Kabbalah* for miraculous acts. But at times, Rabbi Sofer found that he could not excuse himself from such a request.

Leib was a familiar sight among the courtyards in Pressburg.

"Leib, why are you digging through the trash? Do you think you'll find a buried treasure?"

"Leib, have you found any pearls or rubies lately?"

"Leib, is this how a boy who is learning *Gemara* should spend his time?"

Leib just looked up and smiled brightly at the people passing by. Who knows? Maybe he would find something valuable amidst the heaps of trash that lay in the courtyards, something that he could bring back to his good and righteous mother sitting in their large house on Nesterhoiz Street.

Comments? He was used to hearing comments. You couldn't fill your belly with comments, and they wouldn't poison you either. Anyway, he would just look through one more pile. Maybe among the discarded bricks, twisted metal bars, plaster, candle drippings and shattered china he would find something special, something that he could sell for a few coins, something that perhaps he could take home and show his mother. Just one more pile, and then he would go home and learn *Gemara* with his tutor, Rabbi Moshe Pappenheim.

Leib the charming, Leib the lively boy, Leib with the sparkle in his eyes leaned over the broken trash and reached a hand down to sift through it. Suddenly, a vacuum seemed to invade his belly. There was a struggle inside him, as though some malevolent force was climbing into him. Leib tried to straighten up, he tensed his stomach muscles, trying to force the spirit out. He wanted to move, he wanted to open his lips and cry out, "*Shema Yisrael!*" but he was paralyzed. It was as though he was trapped in deep water, far below the surface. At the top was sanity, normality, sunshine, but here, under the surface, he was caught, wrestling with an enormous malevolent force that was poisoning him, filling him with cold and hatred.

I'll . . . I'll just try to move my lips, Leib thought. If I can only move my lips a little, then I'll snap out of it. Then I'll be free. Oh, G-d, help me! But the thought was washed away in a flood of frigidity that overcame him. Leib's consciousness fled his heart and thoughts, fled his senses, fled his limbs, and took refuge in the dim recesses of his mind. The other power, angry, vile, and completely self-centered, spread throughout his limbs, spread across his heart, washed over his mind.

Minutes after Leib had bent over, he straightened up again, thrusting his shoulders back defiantly. His face was twisted into a scowl. He swaggered home, casting angry, arrogant looks at the people who greeted him, kicking rocks out of his way, spitting contemptuously when he passed the synagogue.

Leib's mother heard him enter the house and breathed a sigh of relief.

"Leib? Are you here? I was starting to get worried, it's late. Please try to come home earlier. Leib, why don't you answer me? Are you all right? What's wrong?"

She worriedly came out of the bedroom. What was all that noise from the study room? What could be wrong?

She stopped suddenly in the hall, staring in horror into the room. The *mezuzah* lay cast down to the floor. Leib was standing on the table with a crazy grin on his face. He was ripping the cover off a *Chumash* and throwing it to the floor. All around the desk were scattered ripped-apart *Chumashim*, *siddurim* and the expensive *Gemara* that they owned.

"Leib!" shrieked his mother. "What has come into you?"

"Get lost, you ugly old witch," Leib snarled at his mother. "Go on, get out of here!"

Shrieking in horror, Leib's mother ran into the street, sobbing and crying out.

"What's wrong?" a group of people asked her.

"My Leib!" she brokenly forced out. "He's gone completely mad!"

The group of men and women rushed into the house. They too were stunned by the sight of Leib ripping apart the *sefarim*. "Leib!" one of the men stepped forward. "Put down that *Gemara*!"

Leib threw the *sefer* down. He started jumping about the room like a demented monkey, making strange motions with his hands, and his face turned different shades.

He happened to pass a bookshelf where a secular book was laying. "Ah!" he breathed out. He hugged the book to his bosom, kissed it and crooned over it.

The awful sight of this demented child soon drew people from all over the city. Even priests came to see the young victim. When Leib saw them, he began calling out various names of idolatry, including old names that he could not have ever learned. "Astonishing," they murmured to one another, nodding their tonsured heads. "A most extraordinary instance of possession."

The awful news quickly spread throughout Pressburg. A delegation of rabbis came to Rabbi Sofer. "Please, Rabbi Sofer, you must do something for the boy."

"I am sorry, I am not a miracle worker. We must pray to G-d to have compassion on him."

"But Rabbi Sofer, a *dybbuk* has entered the child. We do not know what to do, but we are sure that you can help. Perhaps G-d desires that you use your abilities in this case!"

Rabbi Sofer sighed. "Very well. Bring the boy to me."

A number of sturdy men were dispatched, and they soon brought the twisting and struggling boy before Rabbi Sofer. They carried him in by his arms and legs and he contorted himself with uncanny energy, trying to break free, a stream of invective coming from his lips as he spit at them.

"Bring the boy here," Rabbi Sofer commanded.

When Leib came before Rabbi Sofer, he calmed down. The men let go of him reluctantly, and he sank down to the floor. Rabbi Sofer bent over and drew the boy between his knees. "Now, son," he said, putting a *Chumash* into the boy's flaccid hands, "learn *Chumash*."

Dutifully, Leib began learning from the *sefer*.

"That's enough," Rabbi Sofer said after a few minutes. He drew the *sefer* out of Leib's hands, and gave the boy a *siddur*. "Now pray from the *siddur*."

The boy opened up the *siddur* and began praying.

"Very well, you may go," Rabbi Sofer said.

Leib stood up, pale and subdued. He slowly walked past the people who were looking on, his gaze cast to the floor, and the people silently parted before him.

"A miracle!" the whispers buzzed. "Extraordinary!"

The boy went out of the *beis midrash* and into the courtyard that stood before the *beis midrash*.

A *minyan* was in the midst of prayer, and through the window, the boy heard the recital of *kedushah* and then *kaddish*. With this, the malignant spirit again entered the defenseless boy and he began leaping about, grimacing and making bizarre motions.

The boy remained in this piteous condition for two more years. He could not tolerate any *sefer* or hearing any words of Torah. He would go down on his knees and call out the names of idols.

Rabbi Sofer did not want to be further involved in the matter. "I will not give the boy a *kemeiah* (amulet)," he told the people who came to speak with him about Leib. "I am a rabbi, not a magician."

But again and again, Rabbi Daniel Prossnitz and other Torah scholars pleaded with Rabbi Sofer to do something for the suffering boy. At last, Rabbi Sofer acquiesced to their pleas.

"Send for Rabbi Fishel Sofer now," he commanded one day.

Someone was immediately dispatched, and he soon came back with Rabbi Fishel Sofer.

Rabbi Sofer handed him a leather sheath that contained a piece of parchment on which Rabbi Sofer had written some words. A string pierced the sheath. "Take this amulet and tie it about the boy's neck," he told him, and he gave him some additional instructions.

Rabbi Fishel Sofer gathered a group of men and sent someone out to get hold of a sack and a black dog.

The group of men, leading the animal, made their way to Leib's house, rehearsing what they would do when they got there.

When they arrived at the house, the men gathered in the courtyard below Leib's window. Meanwhile, Rabbi Fishel Sofer went upstairs by himself. He knocked at the door. Leib's mother, a haggard woman, opened the door. "Yes?" she answered in surprise.

Rabbi Fishel Sofer motioned to her to be quiet. "Where is the boy?" he asked in a low voice.

"In his room."

"Show me his room."

"It's down the hall—the first door on the right."

Rabbi Fishel Sofer quietly went down the corridor. He carefully turned the knob and eased the door open. Leib lay in bed on his back, fully dressed in grimy clothing. His face and hands were dirty, and his hair was long and unkempt.

Rabbi Fishel Sofer took a step forward and the boy glared at him with red-rimmed eyes. Rabbi Fishel Sofer took another step and the boy leaped up from the bed and threw himself at Rabbi Fishel Sofer, kicking and clawing wildly.

Rabbi Sofer whipped the amulet from his pocket and, ignoring the fierce attack of the boy, struggled to tie it about his neck. The boy struggled harder than ever and with both hands pulled the string away from him, cursing Rabbi Fishel Sofer, blaspheming and calling on the names of idols.

Rabbi Fishel Sofer dealt the boy a powerful blow with all his force into the boy's belly. The boy gasped out and bent over, turning ashen-faced, his hands crossing over his belly. Rabbi Fishel Sofer quickly wrapped the string of the amulet about the boy's neck and knotted it tightly.

"Out, out, out, spirit!" he cried hoarsely. "Out, spirit, out! Leave through Leib's little finger, now!"

The boy fell down to the ground and began writhing and screeching, "My hand! My hand!" The flesh and skin of his little finger burst open and blood came gushing out.

Rabbi Fishel Sofer meanwhile ran to the window and raised it wide open. "Spirit, enter the dog!" he yelled.

As soon as he yelled this out, the dog let out an unearthly howl. The men grabbed the animal and thrust it into the sack.

Despite the dog's howls and struggles, the men tied the sack and hurried to the deep, swiftly-flowing Danube River, where they cast it into the water.

The boy lay exhausted on the floor and gradually came to his senses. Within a few days, he was completely healed of the malady of madness that had overcome him. He learned in Rabbi Sofer's *yeshivah* and he eventually grew up to be a fine, G-d-fearing Jew.

Another time, a delegation came to Rabbi Sofer with similar news. "A young boy has begun to act in a strange, uncanny manner. It is evidently a case of a *dybbuk* having entered him. Please have pity on the boy and his mother and father, and use your knowledge of *Kabbalah* to save him."

After much pleading, Rabbi Sofer was persuaded to attend to the boy.

Rabbi Sofer summoned ten of his students who were known for their uncommon piety.

After receiving his instructions, they went to the house of the unfortunate child. They surrounded him in a circle, holding hands tightly. Then they began reciting a number of *Tehillim*, having in mind certain intentions as they did so.

The boy suddenly leaped up from his place and began making all sorts of strange motions. He started yelling and jumping about grotesquely. The students clenched each other's hands, raising their voices and concentrating on the intentions they were supposed to have in mind.

There was a sudden crash. A window pane had shattered. The boy abruptly fell to the ground in exhaustion. The students in the circle about him resolutely continued the ritual as the boy stared dazedly at them.

Then, little by little, the boy regained his health, until he completely recovered.

A few years following the marriage of Rabbi Shmuel Strauss, Rabbi Sofer decided that it was time to marry off the orphan, Ezra, whom he had brought up in his house.

A number of possible connections were mentioned, including the daughter of the wealthy community head of Serdahely, Rabbi Nechemiah. Rabbi Sofer could not decide who would be best for Ezra.

One morning, Rabbi Sofer awoke with the words, "For You, G-d, have helped (in Hebrew, *Ezra*) me, and comforted (in Hebrew, *Nechemiah*) me." Rabbi Sofer immediately sent a message to Rabbi Nechemiah and confirmed the engagement of the boy to Rabbi Nechemiah's daughter.

The wedding took place in Serdahely. Rabbi Sofer met the communal leaders, and they fell to discussing Rabbi Mordechai Banet. Rabbi Sofer mentioned that he and Rabbi Banet had spent a few weeks together in Baden. He said, "In that time, we went through the Talmud and the Jerusalem Talmud, the *Sifra*, the *Sifri*, the *Tosefta*, *Mechilta* and the writings of the Ari." Such a schedule would take an ordinary mortal years to complete—perhaps an entire lifetime.

Rabbi Sofer suddenly fell silent and turned away. He felt that he had revealed too much. It wasn't right, he felt, that others should know of his familiarity with the writings of the Arizal and his involvement in the study of *Kabbalah*.

Rabbi Daniel Prossnitz was also having dreams.

Dark, disturbing, tenebrous and appalling, night after night, the shadowy images, the fleeting horrors, the shocking grotesqueries of image and delusion—these had become the disturbing field of Rabbi Daniel Prossnitz's sleep. His sleep had become a battlefield of terror.

Almost every day, Rabbi Daniel Prossnitz went through the ceremony of the *hatavas chalom* to ameliorate any evil effects his dream might have on waking reality.

"Rabbi," he approached Rabbi Sofer. "These dreams are robbing me of my ability to live. I am constantly trembling. I worry all day. These dreams are overtaking my waking life.

216

Please give me an amulet to protect me from these awful insinuations of evil."

Reluctantly, Rabbi Sofer agreed. "You know it is not my custom to distribute amulets. But because you are such a close friend and because I recognize that you have reached high levels in your apprehension of the world of *Kabbalah*, I will do as you request."

On Friday afternoon, Rabbi Sofer summoned his student, Rabbi Fishel Sofer. "Here is an amulet for Rabbi Daniel Prossnitz. And here is its container." Rabbi Sofer handed Rabbi Fishel Sofer a rolled-up parchment and a leather sheath on a string. "Be sure that when you give Rabbi Daniel Prossnitz the amulet that you tie it into its holder right-side up."

"Yes, Rabbi."

"Be careful. Do not accidently put it in upside-down."

"Of course not."

Rabbi Fishel Sofer went out of Rabbi Sofer's room, holding the amulet and its holder. He put the amulet carefully into the holder and sealed it. Then he hurried down the streets of Pressburg.

"Rabbi Daniel Prossnitz!" Rabbi Sofer knocked at his door. "Rabbi Prossnitz!"

Rabbi Prossnitz came to the door. "Rabbi Fishel! Please come in."

"Thank you, I cannot. But here is the amulet from Rabbi Sofer. Just tie it around your neck."

Rabbi Prossnitz took the amulet from Rabbi Fishel Sofer and gingerly slipped it over his head.

On *Shabbos* morning, before *Kiddush*, Rabbi Sofer went to the outhouse. Unknown to him, his small son Yuzpa ran after him. When Rabbi Sofer left, he closed the door behind him, locking in his son.

As Rabbi Sofer sat down to his meal, he realized that his son was missing. "Where is Yuzpa?" People started searching all around. Where had the boy disappeared to? People began panicking.

Finally, someone heard a bitter voice crying from the outhouse, where he had been locked in.

Rabbi Sofer was very upset by the entire episode, and he said, "I knew that they would give me no rest."

He immediately called for Rabbi Fishel Sofer. "Did you insert the amulet in its case upside-down?"

"I did exactly as you told me to," replied Rabbi Fishel.

"No, you put it in upside-down."

"I am sure that I did only what you said."

"Go tell Rabbi Prossnitz to take off the amulet."

"But Rabbi—"

"Without arguments, please."

When *Shabbos* was over, Rabbi Sofer called in Rabbi Fishel. "Here is the amulet. I am going to open it up. Now look carefully." Rabbi Sofer drew the parchment out of the amulet and unfolded it. The writing was upside-down.

"But Rabbi—how did you possibly know?"

"Why do you ask me that, Rabbi Fishel? Even if I were to tell you, you still wouldn't understand."

31

The Yeshivah Under Attack

THE STRUGGLE BETWEEN THE FORCES OF ORTHODOXY AND REFORM was fierce and unrelenting. It was a conflict that the gentile government did not hesitate to enter. In 1823, the Orthodox side was heartened when the government issued a decree ordering Jews to worship "according to the traditional ritual, without the least innovations in language, ceremonies, prayers and liturgy." This meant the outlawing of Reform temples.

But the Reform forces were not quiescent. In 1825, another school teaching secular studies was opened in Pressburg.

Then, the Reform leaders hit upon a bold and daring strategy. They would attack Rabbi Sofer's center of power, his *yeshivah* with its hundreds of loyal students. They would influence the government to force Rabbi Sofer to close his famed *yeshivah*.

Quickly, the leaders of the Reform movement went to work. Their tools were deceit and cozenage, sharp practice and cunning. Their strategy was treachery; their purpose foul play. Soon their strategy, black as the heart of darkness, was set in motion.

Men of smooth faces and crooked hearts, men of facile words and ugly thoughts insinuated their way into the corridors of gentile power. In the drawing rooms of the aristocrats, in the parlors of the ruling forces, these self-appointed representatives of Judaism wed their hatred toward tradition to the ruling class's antipathy toward Torah in an unholy and destructive alliance.

With smooth tongues, their pates shining in the candlelight of the exclusive chambers of the powerful, they poured out their subtle poison as though bestowing nectar.

"The *yeshivah* of Rabbi Sofer is reactionary! It shall keep the Jews separate and disloyal. It teaches superstition and corruption, hypocrisy and cant. We who love light cannot tolerate the dark. The Jews of Hungary must be brought to the nineteenth century through an enlightened education that will open their eyes to the benevolence of their rulers."

Their words were whispered in the parlors, bandied from court official to court official, spoken openly at dinners, discussed seriously at convocations, weighed and considered. And finally the voice of the government, the imperial will, the royal representative of Hungary, spoke. In 1825, the *yeshivah* of Pressburg was ordered to close its doors.

But the battle was not so quickly won. The government was still not sufficiently under the sway of the Reform activists, and it did not enforce its decree.

A year later, the further agitation of the Reform leadership bore fruit. The governor-general of Pressburg sent a questionnaire with ten questions regarding the activities of the *yeshivah* to Rabbi Sofer.

But Rabbi Sofer replied to the governor's satisfaction, and the governor refused to acquiesce to the Reform advocates and close the *yeshivah*.

The industry of these Reform advocates was admirable, however. They did not falter nor pause in their single-minded aim to bring down the *yeshivah* of Pressburg.

Another year passed, and the Reform advocates hurried through palaces and government offices, negotiated, lobbied, campaigned, made alliances and promises, engineered agreements and associations. Finally, in 1827, an imperial decree was issued: the *yeshivah* of Pressburg must close its doors within fourteen days.

Rabbi Sofer himself went to the Reform leader who was the prime instigator in this campaign and pleaded for the cause of the *yeshivah*, the cause of Torah, for the right of Jews to inherit their own tradition. But the man was adamant and he rebuffed Rabbi Sofer. This Reformer stood for progress, for enlightenment and for civility. And for their sake he was prepared, no, he was eager and ready to destroy. If the cause, the great and enlightened cause that would lead all humanity to bliss, demanded sacrifices, demanded carnage—well, what better proof of his commitment to progress than this, that he was ready to pay for utopia by bringing about ruination?

Rabbi Sofer returned to his community with a heavy heart. After the community leaders talked over the matter, it was decided that the only way to forestall the closure of the *yeshivah* was to appeal to the flexible conscience of the royal government through the means of a sizable bribe.

Two wealthy members of the community, Moshe Bettelheim and Wolf Pappenheim, agreed to pool together the vast fortune of 20,000 gulden. This amount was paid to the government, and the government, satisfied with its gains, nodded its gracious head and allowed the *yeshivah* to continue its existence.

Rabbi Sofer's health, always precarious, suffered as a result of this episode. His hair began turning white and he lost a great deal of his strength.

At the same time that Jewish Reformers were attempting to destroy the connection between Jews and *halachah*, gentile attitudes regarding social change in general and their attitudes toward Jewish rights in particular were becoming more liberal and humane. As a result, the period from 1825 to 1867 became known as the "Reform Period." The question of Jewish political status became a frequent topic of discussion in the legislature, the newspapers and other such forums.

Some believed that Jews should immediately be given unconditional civil rights. Others said that Jews should be granted civil rights only after they had reformed their social and religious practices; and still a third group believed that they should never be granted civil rights.

Thus, the Jews' ability to gain civil rights was linked by many to a belief that the Jews should reciprocate by "reforming" their way of life—that is, by weakening their commitment to Torah and *halachah*.

As a result, many Jews came to believe that in order for Jews to remain loyal to the Torah, it was necessary that they continue to be harassed, persecuted and permanently second-class citizens.

Although the architects of the Reform movement did not succeed in closing the *yeshivah* of Pressburg, they remained eager to weaken it. In the same year, they proposed the opening of a school for small children, where the bulk of the learning would consist of secular learning, with only a modest amount of time set aside for Torah.

The supporters of this program included a number of powerful and wealthy Jews, who sided with the politically crafty Reform advocate, Aaron Chorin.

Rabbi Sofer responded to this threat to the sovereignty of

Torah by delivering a heartfelt and impassioned speech in the synagogue. He spoke movingly about the requirement to follow Torah, and he warned that G-d would punish those who violated His will. His words made a great impression on the people.

More than that, over the course of the following year, his words were proven to be prophetic. One by one, all the leaders of this Reform enterprise met strange deaths. One man grew sick and died. Another hanged himself. A third drowned in the river.

One of these men, upon seeing this chain of events, escaped to Vienna. From his refuge there, he wrote to Rabbi Sofer, begging his forgiveness and asking Rabbi Sofer to pray for him.

Rabbi Sofer commented, "I certainly have this man in my prayers. Whenever I recited *Velamalshinim*—let there be no hope for the informers." Soon afterwards, this man died as well.

But Rabbi Sofer felt no joy in the downfall of his enemies. And he would never petition G-d to punish them.

At that time, two Torah scholars who were close to Rabbi Sofer came to him as he was learning *Sanhedrin*. They asked him, "Why don't you reveal your strength and overthrow these wicked men, these enemies of G-d and Torah? We know very well of your powers and that you can bring about judgement to fall on the heads of these evil men. If you do this, you will not only give them what they truly deserve, but you will sanctify the name of Heaven, for all the people will see that those who fight against the Torah meet a crushing end."

Rabbi Sofer replied, "Believe me, with the power of learning this *Tosafos*"—he pointed to a *Tosafos* on the page of his *Gemara*—"I could uproot them entirely. I know that G-d will carry out the will of those who fear Him. But I do not want to do such a thing. It does not seem right to me that I should be the cause of punishment. But G-d will act for Himself and bring them to judgement."

Rabbi Sofer was not able to prevent the opening of this school. In subsequent writings, he referred bitingly to the organizers of this school as heretics who had cut themselves loose from Jewish tradition.

But the leaders of the Reform movement were not in mourning. To the contrary, they were in the midst of celebrating. They were greeting a new dawn and turning their backs on what they believed to be the benighted, cloying obligations of an old world. Soon they abrogated the fast of *Tishah b'Av* and instead organized a feast on that day. They were, after all, men who knew true joy in life. They were the men of the future!

While the Chasam Sofer could not destroy the Reform leaders or the Reform movement, he did guarantee that a staunch and vibrant Orthodoxy would continue to flourish for future generations.

32

Episodes of Exile

RABBI SOFER WAS TROUBLED. THE LETTER HE HAD RECEIVED LAY upon his desk. The writing was spiked and somewhat tremulous, blotched—perhaps by spilled water, perhaps by a tear.

His mother had written him. She had reminded him that she had not seen him for some years. Now she wrote with a pathos that cut to the depth of his heart. She would like him to visit her so that she could see him once again before she died.

What should he do? If his mother called to him, then he should get up and hasten to see her. He should leave tonight and travel without stopping. It was his obligation as a son.

But then again, he was Rabbi of Pressburg. He was head of and a teacher in the *yeshivah*, leader of the fight against the Reform movement. He was constantly answering *halachic* queries, constantly helping others, constantly advising the community. He was in charge of distributing charitable funds, and he was in charge of a thousand other details of life that affected not only Pressburg but communities all over Central Europe. How could he take himself away from all this?

Once he left, it would be at least several weeks—perhaps a month—before he would be able to return. Could he set aside his responsibilities?

On the one hand, he was bound by the obligation to honor his mother. On the other, he was obliged to remain where he was as a teacher of Torah.

Rabbi Sofer did not trust himself to answer this question himself. He put the question to some Torah scholars, and they replied that his obligation to teach Torah took precedence.

Rabbi Sofer immediately dispatched Rabbi Ber Frank to visit his mother in order to see how she was and to give her news about him.

As Chief Rabbi of Pressburg, Rabbi Sofer came into contact with a variety of Jews. Although he himself did not have *Chassidic* leanings, in his role as Chief Rabbi of Pressburg he came into contact with several of the greatest *Chassidic* leaders of Hungary and Galicia.

In addition, Rabbi Sofer's influence spread as far as the Land of Israel, for the Jews of Jerusalem turned to Rabbi Sofer when they had a dispute over the allocation of funds.

These Jews were supported by charitable funds raised in Europe. Two groups—one *Chassidic* and one non-*Chassidic*— were arguing over the apportionment of this money. Each group claimed that it was being deprived of its fair share.

In his letter to Jerusalem, Rabbi Sofer wrote, "In my humble opinion, all Jews are equal, all Jews are brothers, *chassidim* or non-*chassidim*, and I do not know of any basis for making such distinctions between Jews."

In appreciation of Rabbi Sofer's involvement in this case, he was sent a piece of wood cut from what is believed to be the tree under which Abraham seated the three angels when they came to visit him.

Rabbi Sofer gave the piece of wood to a carpenter. He instructed him, "Carve this into a handle and place into it this circumcision blade." That blade was the scalpel with which Rabbi Adler had circumcised Rabbi Sofer. The handle was plated with pure silver, on which was engraved the verse, "And behold, three men were standing by him."

Rabbi Sofer said that from the time he began to use this knife to perform circumcisions, there were never any complications.

Rabbi Sofer had very passionate feelings about the holiness of the Land of Israel, and a number of his students left Europe to go live in the Holy Land. Rabbi Sofer pointed out that "The essence of the observance of Torah and *mitzvos* is only in the land of life, which is the Land of Israel."

He wrote that "All of our exile was decreed because we insulted the Land of Israel, saying that 'It is a land that consumes its inhabitants.' As a result, we were forced to suffer weeping for generations." Rabbi Sofer therefore stressed the importance of not speaking badly about the Land of Israel.

Rabbi Sofer contrasted the state of the Land of Israel with that of other lands. Our sages teach that "One hour of repentance and good deeds in this world is better than the entire World-to-Come." Rabbi Sofer pointed out that "This statement refers only to the Land of Israel, but not to an unclean land."

In 1830, Rabbi Moshe Zaks was the first of his students to emigrate to the Land of Israel. Other students followed over the next fifty years. Although a number of the followers of the Baal Shem Tov and the followers of the Vilna Gaon moved to the Land of Israel en masse, the students of Rabbi Sofer went to Israel as individuals.

Rabbi Sofer felt strongly that Jews moving to the Land of Israel should earn their own keep. He wrote, "It is forbidden to go to the Land of Israel in order to live off charity. When such a person moves there, he steals from the impoverished Jews who already are living there and who themselves depend on charity." He was also in favor of Jews engaging in farming. Many of his students who emigrated to the Land of Israel helped establish and develop agricultural settlements.

Meanwhile, the land of exile burned beneath the feet of its inhabitants.

"Fire! Fire!" The cry rang out one day in the streets of Pressburg.

"Where?"

"Don't you see? Up there at the top of Schlossburg Hill."

The man looked up to see smoke billowing out of a window. "That—that's Rabbi Sofer's house!"

People rushed out of their houses and ran up the hill to extinguish the conflagration. But there was no water. Because it was difficult to dig a well on top of a hill, very few wells had been built there.

People raced about in blind confusion. The flames would soon race through Rabbi Sofer's house and then spread to the adjoining houses. By nightfall, half of the Jewish section of Pressburg might be engulfed in flames and ruin.

But what could they do if there was no water?

Before Rabbi Sofer's house stood a rusted, disused hand pump. Many years earlier, when Rabbi Meshullam Tismenitzer had lived there, he had built a *mikveh* in his basement, and people had drawn water for their needs from the *mikveh*. But Rabbi Sofer used the communal *mikveh*, and so the *mikveh* in his house had been allowed to go dry.

Now, in the midst of the tumult, a young man caught sight of the hand pump. Not knowing that it was broken, he began to pump the handle, and water gushed out. "Water, water!" a cry went up. The people gathered in a line, passing bucket after bucket from the freely flowing hand pump to extinguish the fire, and the blaze was quickly put out.

"That's odd," people mused after the fire was over. "We always assumed that the hand pump hadn't been working. It goes to show, if you don't try, you don't know."

"That's really good news. It will really be convenient not to have to carry water up from down the hill."

But when someone tried the water pump again, it creaked emptily and remained dry. Again—but it was bone-dry. There was not a drop of water. Then the news went through the crowd, "G-d created a miracle to put out the fire in Rabbi Sofer's house."

33

Family Affairs

REIZL SOFER, MOTHER OF RABBI SOFER, HAD *DAVENED MINCHAH* IN the synagogue with a *minyan*, as was her custom.

She walked home slowly, her small, wrinkled fingers clutching the ends of the kerchief about her dainty pale face.

She came into her house, and called her daughter-in-law.[2]

"Chuldah, please come with me to my room. There is something I wish to tell you."

Chuldah followed the form of her mother-in-law through the apartment to Mrs. Sofer's room. Reizl sat down on her bed. "Chuldah, today has come my time to leave this world."

---

[2] The widow of the Chasam Sofer's brother Yuzpa, who died in 1821, about a year before his mother. Of Chuldah, his sister-in-law, the Chasam Sofer always spoke very highly, when he needed to give her *chalitzah* she travelled all the way to Pressburg, rather than cause him to lose time from his learning and teaching.

"Mama, what are you saying?"

"Quiet, child. My time has come to leave the world today. Bring me my shrouds to put on, and call the righteous women here, so they can be with me when I leave."

Chuldah stood in place, trembling.

"There is no need to tremble, my dear," Reizl said gently. "Do as I tell you. Bring me my shrouds and call the women."

"Mama!" Chuldah burst out again, breaking into tears.

"Do as I say, child," Reizl repeated patiently. "Bring me my shrouds and bring the women."

Chuldah left the room to do her mother-in-law's bidding.

When the women came to Reizl's bed, she was lying down peacefully, dressed in her shrouds. In the presence of the women who had gathered with her, she recited a few prayers, and in the midst of her prayers died peacefully.

Later, when Rabbi Sofer learned of his mother's death, he said in his grief, "G-d, You told me ahead of time everything you intended to do. But this You hid from me."

The wheel of life continued to turn. Avraham Shmuel, Rabbi Sofer's oldest son, was engaged to be married. The dowry had been set at ten thousand gulden, and the wedding date was drawing close.

But Rabbi Sofer heard disturbing news about his son's fiancee. On the eve of the fast of the tenth of *Teves*, she had gone to the theater. This insensitivity disturbed him deeply, and he returned the dowry and broke off the engagement.

The young woman soon afterwards became engaged to a wealthy man, and the wedding was performed by Rabbi Sofer. When he covered her face with a veil before she went beneath the canopy, he recited the traditional blessing in an unusually loud voice.

Later, a number of people asked Rabbi Sofer why he had blessed her so loudly.

Rabbi Sofer replied, "I know that because of the broken

engagement to my son, this woman will be punished by Heaven. If I had blessed her in a whisper, people would have said that I was cursing her."

Not long afterward, the woman contracted a disease that made it impossible to continue leading a married life. She divorced her husband—with Rabbi Sofer taking care of the ceremony—and remained unmarried for the rest of her life.

One day, Rabbi Pinchas Leib fell sick. In his youth, Rabbi Sofer had encouraged him to begin learning when others of his age were already accomplished scholars. Now he was a learned rabbi, and the study-partner of Rabbi Meir Asch.

Rabbi Pinchas Leib lay on his deathbed, surrounded by the members of the *chevrah kaddisha*, among whom was Rabbi Meir Asch.

There was noise at the door, and Rabbi Sofer entered.

"Please leave the room," he ordered preemptorily.

Without a murmur, the *chevrah kaddisha* members got up and filed out the door. But Rabbi Meir Asch stepped to the side and hid behind a long window curtain.

From behind the curtain, he heard Rabbi Sofer ask Rabbi Pinchas Leib, "Do you see?"

"Yes," came Rabbi Pinchas Leib's reply.

There was a long silence. Then again, Rabbi Meir Asch heard Rabbi Sofer ask, "Do you see?" And Rabbi Pinchas Leib again replied, "Yes."

There was another long span of silence—and then the same enigmatic question and answer.

This went on for the course of the next hour.

Finally, Rabbi Sofer left the room.

Immediately afterwards, Rabbi Pinchas Leib began to recover, and in a few days, he was completely well.

A few days later, Rabbi Meir Asch asked Rabbi Pinchas Leib, "Tell me what happened when you were sick and Rabbi Sofer visited you."

"I'm sorry. I can't do that."

"Then do me this favor. When you go to Rabbi Sofer to get his blessing for your health, let me come along, so I can hide and overhear your conversation."

"Well . . . all right."

Some time afterwards, Rabbi Pinchas Leib entered Rabbi Sofer's room, and Rabbi Meir Asch secreted himself outside the door. He leaned against the wall and strained to hear what the two men were saying inside. He could barely make out Rabbi Pinchas Leib's voice when, during the course of his visit, he asked, "Rabbi, what did you mean when you asked me if I see anything?"

"Well, what did you see?" Rabbi Meir Asch heard Rabbi Sofer reply.

"I thought I saw an awesome, old man come into the room and stand at the right side of my bed. It seemed to me that he was Avraham Avinu. Then another awesome man came in—it seemed to me that he was Yitzchak Avinu—and he stood at his father's right side. Then a third great man walked in, whom I took to be Yaakov Avinu, and he stood at his father's left side. After that, three more men entered and stood on the left side of my bed. I imagined that they were Moshe, Aharon and David Hamelech.

"Then they began arguing whether or not I should continue to live. Finally, a seventh man walked into the room, dressed in linen. I took him to be Eliyahu Hanavi.

"He listened to them arguing, and then he pointed a finger at you and said that your merit was enough to stand by me and save my life. And from that point on, I began to recover."

Outside the door, Rabbi Meir Asch listened in awe and amazement. Was Rabbi Sofer a human being or an angel? Could he even begin to gauge the greatness of Rabbi Sofer's measure?

34

Emancipation

EMANCIPATION! THAT SWEET WORD WAS ON THE LIPS OF THE JEWS of Pressburg. Equality, freedom from persecution, the ability to earn a decent wage. The hopes ran through their veins like sweet wine.

The government ministers were meeting in the Parliament in Pressburg to discuss the status of the Jews, and they were close to giving the Jews civil rights.

Pressburg's communal leaders approached Rabbi Sofer and told him that they thought it would be fitting and politically astute to give public thanks for the good that these government officials were doing for the Jews.

That *Shabbos*, Rabbi Sofer gave a talk in the large synagogue. At the end of his sermon, he told the following parable:

A king ruled over a great country. He had a son whom

he loved a great deal and in whom he placed all his trust to one day take over the rulership.

But his son fell into bad company and acted badly against both G-d and man.

The king grew deeply disturbed. He rebuked his son, but his son did not take his words to heart.

The king then sent his ministers to speak to his son. But nothing helped. The son blithely continued his unprincipled way of life.

When the king saw that his son would not change his ways, he expelled him to live in a far-off land in the house of a peasant who would support him with the barest of means.

The son lived in that barren outpost many years.

Finally, the king began to feel sorry for his son. He decided that he would build his son a beautiful palace. He sent architects and builders to his son, together with many servants and a gift of a great deal of money.

When this great entourage arrived, the king's son was ecstatic. But his joy soon turned to grief. If his father had spent so much money to send all these people to him, his father evidently must intend for him to remain there for a very long time.

The son's heart was broken, and he wrote his father, "My dear father: I am very happy that you thought of me and sent people to build a palace for me. But I am sick at heart, because I realize that you mean for me to remain here a long time. Until now, I had hoped every day that you would take me back home. But now I see that I was wrong. So I am asking you to have mercy and let me come back to you."

The king, Rabbi Sofer explained, is G-d, the King of the Universe, Who chose us from all the nations. He is our Father, and we are His children.

We were at His table, in His palace—that is, in the Land of Israel.

We sinned and abandoned G-d's ways, until G-d sent us His

ministers—that is, His prophets—to warn us. However, we didn't take their rebuke to heart, but continued sinning, against both G-d and our fellow man.

Finally, G-d expelled us from the Land of Israel.

In this terrible exile, we barely kept alive, and we cried out to G-d to bring us back to our land.

Now, G-d has had compassion on us, and the nation in which we live has considered emancipating us and giving us equal rights.

This is truly a great favor, and we are very thankful for it, insofar as our physical well-being is concerned.

But our souls are in mourning, for this means that the King intends that we will remain here a long time, and we shall never return to the Land of Israel.

So what place is there for joy? Only in our own land does the true blessing lie: the spiritual blessing of eternal life, in the place of the Beis Hamikdash, the *mizbayach*, the *kohein*, the *aron* and the *Sanhedrin*.

Rabbi Sofer cried out bitterly, "*Rabbosai*, I can no longer hold myself back. I must challenge G-d. Why should a father exile His sons? What more does G-d want?

"Happy is the King Who is praised with Torah and prayer, whether it be in His own house or in a foreign land. But woe to the sons who are exiled from the table of their Father.

"G-d, You sit on Your throne for all generations and lack nothing. But why do You forget us forever? Why do You abandon us for so long?"

Rabbi Sofer burst into tears, and the hearts of all the people in the crowded synagogue broke. "My brothers," Rabbi Sofer concluded, "let us pray to our Father in heaven, 'Please have mercy on us. Bring us back to our own land, where we will be close to our Father's table.' G-d will not expel us forever. The Eternal One of Israel will not be false, and a redeemer shall return to Zion."

Rabbi Sofer's feeling of exile was profound. He wrote, "Our eyes see that most *mitzvos* are not fulfilled properly because we live among gentiles."

Elsewhere, he said, "How shall we not be sorrowful and mourn? We have cried out to G-d for the loss of our money, which we could not bear—but are we able to bear the loss of our Holy Land and the place where G-d's presence dwelt?

"If we had rest in the land of the gentiles and the governments were kind to us, we would not seek redemption. Yet this is our entire desire—to get close to the gentiles and hope that they will be pleased with us and we will become like them, G-d forbid."

In these words, Rabbi Sofer expressed his deep awareness of the curse of exile. Political emancipation, he stressed, though a blessing for the Jews' physical existence, is no substitute for their spiritual release from exile.

35

Family Life

"A WOMAN OF VALOR, WHO CAN FIND, FOR HER WORTH IS BEYOND precious stones."

Line by line, Rabbi Sofer read Shlomo Hamelech's tribute to the woman of valor in a choked voice.

He interpreted each line as referring to his wife of twenty-one years. At the age of forty-two, in 5592 (1832), her holy soul had left this world and returned to the garden of its eternal home.

After his eulogy, Rabbi Sofer read aloud the will that his wife had written some years earlier. In her will, she asked that Rabbi Sofer forgive her for not having taken as good care of him as a man as great as he deserved. She had been unable to do so, she said, because she had suffered so much from disease. She instructed her sons not to fast on her *yahrzeit*, but instead to learn Torah with extra diligence. Finally, she

238

commanded her daughters to encourage their husbands to learn Torah.

In later years, Rabbi Avraham Shmuel used to complete a tractate of *Gemara* every year on his mother's *yahrzeit* so that he could eat a festive meal. However, he only had dairy food, and not meat at that meal.

Soon Rabbi Sofer was approached with names of candidates for marriage, for people felt that he could not live alone. Rabbi Sofer said that he would marry only after his eldest son Rabbi Avraham Shmuel, who was then sixteen, would be married.

Soon thereafter, in that same year, Rabbi Avraham Shmuel married Leah, the daughter of Rabbi Yitzchak Weiss of Gorlitz.

Rabbi Avraham Shmuel's father-in-law committed himself to supporting the young man for six years. The newly-wed couple settled in Pressburg, and for the first year of their marriage, they ate in the house of Rabbi Sofer. During this six-year period, Rabbi Avraham Shmuel learned a phenomenal amount of Torah.

Two young students learned with him in his house. He would go to sleep in the evening, while they stayed up. At midnight, they would wake him. He would rise, say *tikkun chatzos* and learn until *Shacharis*.

When he felt sleep overtaking him, he would go out to the porch to wake up. Sometimes he was so exhausted that he would have to prop his eyelids open with his fingers.

Rabbi Avraham Shmuel would learn through the lectures that his father had delivered in the *yeshivah*. In addition to this, he maintained his own learning schedule.

Rabbi Sofer would show his son questions that he received in the mail and have him study them. At times, before Rabbi Sofer sent out an answer to a question, he would have Rabbi Avraham Shmuel write his own response. Then they would compare the replies that they had written. In this way,

Rabbi Sofer trained his son in the methodology of clarifying *halachah*. At the end of each week, Rabbi Avraham Shmuel answered letters that had been addressed to him.

Whenever a Torah scholar came to Rabbi Sofer and asked for official permission to grant *halachic* decisions, Rabbi Sofer first had Rabbi Avraham Shmuel test the man.

In addition to his regular learning schedule, Rabbi Avraham Shmuel learned *mussar* literature and classic works of Jewish philosophy. In addition, Rabbi Sofer sometimes sent him works of *Kabbalah* to study. Rabbi Sofer once told his son, "Do not learn Rambam's Guide to the Perplexed until you are forty years old, when you have learned most of the Talmud and you are familiar with *Kabbalah*."

Rabbi Avraham Shmuel was a very private figure in those years. He kept himself separate from most people, associating only with other rabbinical leaders and a few of his father's most outstanding students.

Rabbi Sofer was very proud of his son's learning. He once told some of his close students, "I am sure that an angel has been teaching my son Torah."

Another time, he told some Torah scholars, "My son learns better than I. It is true that he does not know as much as I, but that is only because I am older."

Rabbi Sofer trained his son carefully to be a Torah giant in all his ways, offering himself as a model for his son to emulate.

All of Rabbi Sofer's actions and words, even his casual conversation, were measured carefully.

Rabbi Sofer used to go walking in a public garden near his home with his sons and colleagues. Once he sat down on a bench to rest and the others stood before him. Meanwhile, Rabbi Avraham Shmuel and a friend walked back and forth, discussing a point of Torah.

As they approached Rabbi Sofer, he called out, "My dear son, you are discussing Torah, and you may think that I am discussing empty matters. I want you to know that you will not hear me say a word from which you cannot learn something—if not for now, then for the future."

From that moment, Rabbi Avraham Shmuel became aware that he gained from everything that his father said.

Rabbi Sofer also told his son, "Believe me that I do not take an object from one place and put it someplace else without having a reason for doing so."

Everything that Rabbi Sofer did had a basis in the Torah. He used to interpret the verse that a Torah scroll "should be with the king of Israel and he should read it all the days of his life" as meaning that the king should cling to the Torah and always have it on his mind. Then he will find in it references to whatever happens to him. As a result, all his actions will be based on the Torah.

Rabbi Sofer admonished his children and students that "G-d has only the four cubits of *Halachah*." This, he said, means that every four steps a person takes should be based on *Halachah*. He interpreted the word cubit—*amah*—as being related to the word mother, or source—*eim*, as in the statement, "there is a source—*eim*—to Torah." These four sources are: learning Torah, teaching Torah, guarding Torah and keeping Torah.

Rabbi Sofer once noted, "For over forty years, I have not neglected the teaching of Torah for even one day."

In Rabbi Sofer's view, the teaching of Torah was greater than the building of the Beis Hamikdash and an even greater obligation than honoring one's parents.

Learning Torah, in his view, is the raison d'etre of every Jew. "Even if a person does all the *mitzvos*," Rabbi Sofer declared in one of his talks, "nevertheless, if he does not toil in Torah, we must suspect that he may be tainted by some bit of heresy."

Rabbi Sofer was also careful to append his approbation

only to works which he had time to read.

In 1831, he gave his *haskamah* to a *sefer* written by his student, Rabbi Eliezer Horowitz. This *sefer* was written in German for the benefit of those who did not read Hebrew fluently. In his introduction, Rabbi Sofer pointed out that before giving his approval, he had read through the entire work.

That same year, Rabbi Sofer was sick and suffered a great deal for a long time. Although he recovered, his hair turned white, and he suffered pains and illnesses for the rest of his life. This did not induce him, however, to slacken in his Torah learning and prayer.

One evening, Rabbi Sofer had an unsettling experience.

"The house needs guarding!" Rabbi Sofer's deceased wife had come to him in a vision with these cryptic words.

Rabbi Sofer deciphered them to mean that he must re-marry.

In 5595 (1835), he married the widow of the great scholar Rabbi Tzvi Hirsch Heller, author of *Tiv Gittin*.

Rabbi Sofer's new wife was a holy and wise woman. She said that although her first husband had been extremely holy and pious, she had never experienced such piety as that of Rabbi Sofer.

When Rabbi Sofer was feeling ill, his sons would try to persuade him not to teach. But his wife would tell him not to interrupt his teaching schedule, but that "those who hope in G-d renew their strength." Then he would go and teach.

Throughout his life, Rabbi Sofer suffered from ill health. At times, he was so weak that he did not have the strength to give his lessons himself or to write down his Torah thoughts himself. Once Rabbi Meir Asch said that for thirty or forty years, he had prayed every day, stretched out on the floor, for Rabbi Sofer to have a long life.

Rabbi Sofer was generally very strong. Once, toward the

end of his life, he sat at the head of a committee of Pressburg's communal leaders. He was trying to institute a ruling, and one of the people present disagreed with him. Rabbi Sofer argued with him and he hit the table, which was made of thick, strong wood. The power of his blow splintered the edge of the table.

Every summer, in accordance with his doctor's wishes, Rabbi Sofer went for a few months' vacation to the mineral baths to recuperate from his grinding schedule.

Before leaving for the spa, Rabbi Sofer would be visited by members of the community, who would ask him for his blessing. On *Shabbos*, the community leaders would come to his home.

Then, when Rabbi Sofer left, the community leaders accompanied him out of the city.

If Rabbi Sofer went to a nearby spa, the community rented two carriages. These stood ready from morning till evening to give a ride to any scholar or outstanding student who wished to visit him.

A number of times, Rabbi Sofer went to the baths in Baden, near Vienna.

He used to stroll through the large park near the baths. One year, Ferdinand I, who was then Crown Prince of the Austrian Empire, was also staying in Baden, and he also used to walk through the park.

Ferdinand noticed Rabbi Sofer on his daily walks, and he was struck by his wise and noble features, and he gazed at him for a long while. As the two men strolled back and forth on the sunny, tree-lined path, they kept passing each other. Every time they did so, Ferdinand took especial notice of Rabbi Sofer.

This continued day after day. Finally, Ferdinand met a man from Eisenstadt and asked him, "Who is that rabbi with such a holy face who walks through the park every day?"

"That is Rabbi Sofer, the rabbi of Pressburg."

"Really. It would be interesting to get to know him."

Someone came to Rabbi Sofer to inform him that the Crown Prince was interested in getting to know him, and Rabbi Sofer immediately returned to Pressburg.

In his later years, Rabbi Sofer's income declined. One summer, he decided not to go to the baths. His sons asked him, "Father, why are you staying home? You have to take care of your health."

"My sons, when I had money, I used to conduct my life in a royal fashion. But now I do not have the money to do so, and I will not impose on the community to support me."

When the community members of Pishtcan, where Rabbi Sofer usually went to the baths at that time, realized the reason for his absence, they volunteered to pay his expenses.

Meanwhile, the community heads of Pressburg realized that Rabbi Sofer's generosity and large charitable outlays were causing him financial discomfort. They decided that instead of giving him a fixed income, he would be allowed to take whatever he needed from the communal account. Rabbi Sofer was uncomfortable with this, because he was afraid that he might come to spend more than was proper, but the community never questioned any of his expenses.

Besides this, in Rabbi Sofer's later years, some wealthy men of the community provided him with a sedan chair carried by two porters. Two men were constantly on call to carry him from his home to the synagogue or anywhere else.

When Rabbi Sofer would go to a small town to the baths, he would stay in the house of a non-Jew.

One summer, however, when he went to Jergen, a respected Jew asked Rabbi Sofer to stay with him, and Rabbi Sofer agreed.

Soon, Rabbi Sofer was shocked to hear that this man was claiming that Rabbi Sofer was not careful in his observance of *mitzvos*.

Rabbi Sofer called in his servant. "I want you to tell me exactly what this man is saying about me."

The servant stood silent, his head down.

"Speak!"

"I cannot say such an ugly thing in your presence."

But Rabbi Sofer insisted, and the servant repeated the entire incident.

Rabbi Sofer immediately confronted his host. "I am going to the town rabbi, and I want you to come with me."

"But why . . .?"

"We will discuss that when we get there. Are you ready?"

"This is so sudden—and mysterious. But if you insist . . ."

When they came to the town rabbi, Rabbi Sofer repeated what he had heard. "Now I would like this man to testify under oath whether he has been spreading such rumors about me."

"Yes, yes, I fully admit it," said the man unashamedly. "I have no reason to lie."

"Then tell me why you suspected me," Rabbi Sofer insisted.

"Certainly. I happened to look into your room on *Shabbos* during the day, and I saw you begin your meal without making *Kiddush*! Now what kind of Jew eats on *Shabbos* without making *Kiddush*?"

As it happened, it was Rabbi Sofer's custom to make *Kiddush* earlier. But what sin of his had caused him to be slandered so grievously in his old age? Perhaps it was that he had transgressed the statement in the Talmud that a Torah scholar is not allowed to live together with a pious ignoramus. Rabbi Sofer grew upset with himself that he had forgotten this *halachah*.

But later on, Rabbi Sofer cheered himself. He had always worried that the Jews might get bad leaders who would cause the Jews to disappear utterly. "But now," he considered, "G-d has shown me that I was mistaken. G-d gave the Torah to the most brazen of nations. I am an old rabbi, the leader of a great community, and nevertheless, this person suspected me because he saw me doing something that he had never seen his fathers do. If this is the case, those who are faithful to G-d will not pay any attention to any evil leaders, for the strength of the people lies principally in the way of Torah that they received from their fathers."

36

Response to Reform

"AND WHAT IS THE PURPOSE OF YOUR PROJECT, DR. PINNER?" RABBI Sofer asked the German Jew who sat opposite him.

Dr. Pinner cleared his throat and stroked his auburn beard. "The Torah tells us that 'it is your wisdom and understanding in the eyes of the nations.' My intention is to publish the entire Talmud with a facing German translation.

"For centuries, the Christians have made the most heinous claims against the Jews, based on their distortions of what our Talmud says. But now, the wisdom of the Jewish people will be an open book for all mankind to read. Now all people, Jew and gentile alike, will be able to appreciate the marvels of the Jewish tradition."

"Yes," Rabbi Sofer replied, "but what about the *halachos* that restrict teaching Torah to non-Jews? And furthermore, the Talmud is not a simple text. Many statements must be studied in depth to be appreciated. If the Talmud is made available to all, the light-headed and the scholarly alike, people may come to use this translation as a means of ridiculing Torah yet more."

"I am sure that the great Rabbi Nassan Adler of Hanover has considered these arguments as well," Dr. Pinner replied. (Rabbi Nassan Adler of Hanover was a nephew of the Chasam Sofer's teacher. He later became Chief Rabbi in London and authored the commentary *Nesinah Lager*.) "And he has not only agreed to support this project, but he himself is translating the tractates *Yevamos* and *Eiruvin*."

"Indeed?" mused Rabbi Sofer. "If a man of such stature is supporting your project, I am sure that nothing wrong will come of it. I see no reason to withhold my own support." He took out a foolscap and wrote out an approbation for Dr. Pinner.

But Dr. Pinner's claim had been a prevarication. Soon a letter came to Rabbi Sofer from Rabbi Adler stating that he had nothing to do with this project.

Immediately, Rabbi Sofer withdrew his support and published a retraction of his approbation.

Another time, someone wished to translate the *siddur* into German.

"I am sorry, but I cannot support that," said Rabbi Sofer.

"But Rabbi Sofer, a few years ago, you gave your approbation to a *sefer* written in German by Rabbi Ber Frank, teaching *halachah* to women."

"Yes, but that was an altogether different case. There is nothing wrong with using a gentile language to bring people close to Torah, if they are not conversant with Hebrew. But I cannot approve of a work that will encourage people to pray to G-d in anything else but the words that our tradition has given us."

"But doesn't G-d understand all languages?"

"Yes, of course," Rabbi Sofer replied. "But I will give you a parable. Imagine that someone was very sick, and his doctor gave him a prescription of all the medicines that he needs. If the sick man were to take the prescription and crush it, boil it and eat it, it wouldn't do him a bit of good. He has to take it to the pharmacy and get the drugs that he needs.

"The doctor is the group of *Anshei Knesses Hagedolah*, the great sages who are our doctors of the soul. They arranged the prayers in accordance with many hidden intentions that are embedded in the specific Hebrew words. Other languages cannot contain those hidden meanings. The words of prayer are the prescription. When a person prays, he so to speak comes to the pharmacy—to G-d Himself, Who gives the person his medicine and helps him."

As the movement for Reform and assimilation spread, Rabbi Sofer's position became even more firm and decisive. He saw no room for compromise with these people who had declared themselves against traditional Torah values, and expressed his strong belief that Torah-faithful Jews should have nothing to do with them.

Once, Rabbi Sofer gave a parable to explain his stance:

There was a king who had a daughter who was deathly ill. The king sent her to the royal doctors to take care of her.

One day, when the king came to visit his daughter, he saw a doctor standing before her room holding a sword in his hand.

"What are you doing?" the king exclaimed. "You're supposed to be healing my daughter, not standing out here like a soldier!"

"Your Highness," the doctor replied, "please listen. As long as I hoped that I could cure your daughter, I stood at her side and did all I could for her. But now I see that she cannot recover. All I can do now is to stand by her door and keep others away, so that they will not catch her dreadful disease."

Rabbi Sofer explained, "When these Reformers first appeared and began to change customs and to begin all sorts of things that had never been done before, I argued with them. But now, after all these years, I see that there is no point in trying to communicate with them. They are lost to the Torah.

"Instead, I have decided to focus my attention on supporting and guarding those people who are loyal to the Torah. I stand at the door and I keep the Jews who keep Torah from coming into contact with the Reformers. In this way, I can at least keep those who are healthy from being infected by the Reformers."

Rabbi Sofer felt that a clean break must be made between those who are loyal to Torah and those who are not. When some people with Reform tendencies built a temple, they invited Torah-observant Jews to attend their services. But Rabbi Sofer forbade any Torah-observant Jew to enter the temple.

"It is forbidden to have anything to do with these people or to enter their synagogue," he declared. "Imagine there was a king who commanded his ministers to build him a great palace. But he made the condition that this palace should be so beautiful that there should be no place for an outhouse.

"Once, when the king and his ministers were promenading through the park, they came to a far part of the grounds where there was a pile of dirt. The king grew enraged, but one of his ministers replied, 'Your highness, this is because you allowed no outhouses to be built. But if you give us provisions to build special outhouses, both the palace and the grounds will be immaculate.'

"Similarly," Rabbi Sofer explained, "these Reformers have remained in our synagogues and attempted to persuade Torah-observant Jews to abandon their traditional path. This is like having a mound of trash in the midst of the king's palace. Instead, it would be better to separate them and have them congregate in their separate synagogues. Then G-d's palace will be clean."

In a *halachic* letter, Rabbi Sofer declared, "If we had the power, in my opinion, we should thoroughly expel such people from our community. We should forbid anyone to marry into their families so that they do not draw anyone after them. We would be by ourselves and they would be by themselves. At the moment, we cannot do this, because of the government regulations. But it appears to me that this is the *halachah*."

The rush toward Reform and assimilation was torrential. In one generation, hundreds of thousands of Jews were abandoning a history of thousands of years of Torah observance. Rabbi Sofer used to comment on this in his interpretation of the verse, "New things have come of late that your fathers did not foresee."

How could this be? Certainly, Rabbi Sofer said, our forefathers foresaw that every successive generation following the giving of the Torah would decline in learning Torah and fear of G-d. As our sages said, "If the early ones were like angels, we are like human beings."

The answer, Rabbi Sofer explained, is that in general, every generation descends to a certain, predictable degree. But the verse is teaching us that a generation would come that would precipitously plunge the equivalent of ten generations' descent. These are the "new things that have come of late" of which the verse is speaking.

Rabbi Sofer's response to the crises of Reform and assimilation was predicated on vigorous activism. He decried the passivist attitude that Torah Jews must merely be pious and trust in G-d, and that He would fight for them and take care of them.

Rabbi Sofer said, "Avraham Avinu didn't preach only trust in G-d, whereas his brother Charan claimed total trust in G-d.

"When Nimrod threatened to cast both Avraham and Charan into the furnace, Charan trusted that G-d would save him from the fire.

"But this is not what G-d wants. As a result, Charan was burned to a cinder.

"However, it didn't occur to Avraham Avinu that he should sit back and trust in G-d. When he saw the idol worship about him, he did all he could to fight against it. He decided that if he were to be thrown into a furnace as a result, he was content, because it would be for G-d's sake. He didn't just trust that G-d would save him because he was fighting for G-d's sake. And since Avraham was ready to sacrifice himself for the sake of G-d, G-d saved him and overcame his enemies."

37

Final Days

IN 5597 (1837), WHEN RABBI SOFER WAS SEVENTY-FOUR YEARS OLD, he felt that the end of his years was drawing nearer, and he sat down to compose his will.

Rabbi Sofer wrote:

> "Do not join with the evil-doers who have emerged of late and gone far from G-d and His Torah. Do not dwell in their neighborhood, and do not join them in any way.
>
> Do not touch the books of Moses Mendelssohn.
>
> If you keep away from these, you will never stumble.
>
> Learn *Tanach* with *Rashi* and Torah with *Ramban*, and teach your children . . .
>
> If, G-d forbid, you face hunger and poverty, stand firm and do not turn after false gods.
>
> The women should learn books in Yiddish based on *Aggadah*, and nothing else.

253

You are completely forbidden to attend the theater.

May you see G-d's pleasantness and the joy of the rebuilding of the Beis Hamikdash.

If, as is my hope, G-d blesses you with plenty, do not grow proud or treat any decent person disrespectfully. Know that we are the children of Avraham, Yitzchak and Yaakov, the students of Moshe, the servants of David.

Avraham said, I am dust and ashes. Moshe said, And what are we? David said, I am a worm and not a man. And the *Mashiach* will come in the guise of a poor man, riding on a donkey. In light of this, where is there room for haughtiness?

Learn Torah diligently. Organize public learning. Teach that which G-d has given you, using all your strength, and with a pure heart.

Do not change your name, language or clothing to imitate the ways of the gentiles.

Do not worry that I have not left you wealth. The Father of orphans will have mercy on orphans, and He will not abandon you.

Do not make G-d's Torah a crown or a spade to dig with. You should certainly not become travelling preachers for pay. G-d will take care of you in your place.

Do not say that the times have changed. We have an old Father, blessed be He. He does not change and He will not change."

To the beloved community of Pressburg:

"May G-d bless you.

You enabled me to raise thousands of students in Torah and fear of G-d. These students have subsequently spread out across the face of the earth. You supported a *yeshivah* so that all these students had an opportunity to succeed.

Never elect any person who breaks tradition.

Do not allow the post of chief rabbi to remain vacant for more than two years. Choose only a well-known Torah scholar who fears G-d and who is righteous. He should have nothing to do with heretical literature, and he should not give his talks in the gentile language.

Do not be swayed by ulterior motives. Choose a humble man who spreads Torah.

Make no changes in the funds for teaching Torah and the order of studies.

May G-d bless you with wealth and honor and length of days in the fear of G-d and His Torah, until the coming of the *Mashiach*.

My daughters and daughters-in-law, dress modestly. Be sure that those of you who are married do not allow a hair of your head to be seen. You may not wear wigs.

G-d will grant you grace and mercy.

May you raise your children in the way of Torah and serving G-d.

My dear sons and students:

Do not be lax in the *yeshivah* and its curriculum, including its daily public classes—Gemara, *halachah* and *Tosafos*.

I will be very pleased if my dear son, Avraham Shmuel Binyamin, will give the lecture and you heed him, as has been the case until now."

signed the insignificant Moshe.

In the last sentence, Rabbi Sofer was requesting that his son become the head of the *yeshivah*. Because the head of the *yeshivah* had traditionally also held the post of chief rabbi, Rabbi Sofer was apparently recommending that his son become rabbi after him.

One day, Rabbi Sofer's servant saw him rip his clothes in mourning. The servant backed out of the room in shock.

Some days later, the members of Rabbi Sofer's family read the in the newspaper of the passing of Rabbi Akiva Eiger from this world.

"Don't tell Rabbi Sofer!" they whispered to one another. "The news would be too tragic for him to bear."

The servant told how he had seen Rabbi Sofer tearing his garment some days earlier. Reading the paper's account, they realized that Rabbi Sofer had gone into mourning at the very moment that his father-in-law Rabbi Akiva Eiger had passed away.[3]

Rabbi Sofer summoned the heads of the community and asked them to offer Rabbi Avraham Shmuel the honor of eulogizing Rabbi Akiva Eiger. Rabbi Avraham Shmuel wrote the eulogy and he delivered it to his father with a note that read, "I have done as you have commanded me and eulogized my grandfather of blessed memory, but I only did it in writing. But I cannot by any means deliver the eulogy in the great synagogue, for I am not fit to stand in the holy place of my father."

But Rabbi Sofer was persistently training his son to stand in his stead.

That same year, for instance, Rabbi Sofer asked his son to give a talk every *Shabbos* to the *yeshivah* students and other Torah scholars on any topic in the Talmud.

In the summer, Rabbi Avraham Shmuel's six years of support from his father-in-law came to end. From where would his help now come? He wished only to sit and learn, and he did not want to immerse himself in the life of a communal rabbi.

Rabbi Avraham Shmuel wrote a letter to his father. "You, Father, work yourself so hard as rabbi of Pressburg that you must go to the baths every summer. Even now you are not home but recuperating in Jergen. Would it not be better for

---

[3]Rabbi Sofer wrote to his brother-in-law Rabbi Shlomo Birnbaum, rebuking the children of Rabbi Akiva Eiger for not telling him about the passing of their father. In a revealing response, published in *Igros Sofrim*, he apologized and describes in detail the entire Eiger family.

me if I could continue to devote myself only to learning Torah, G-d's divine gift? My father-in-law is here in Pressburg. I don't know how to approach him. What can I tell him? He has been so generous thus far. But I am afraid of what will happen when he ceases to support me. How will I support my wife and children while continuing to nourish my soul by learning Torah? Please, Father, write to my father-in-law and ask him to extend his support to me and my family. I will do my best to be worthy of his kindness."

When Rabbi Sofer received this letter, he immediately wrote back, "I received your letter close to the onset of *Shabbos*. Do not worry about the future, my son. G-d will raise your honor and your throne, and you will be given an important position. Trust in G-d, not in man or circumstance. A man has many thoughts, but the depth of G-d's intentions toward us is only for the good."

At the end of the summer, when Rabbi Sofer returned home, Rabbi Avraham Shmuel was still distraught. He approached his old, white-haired father in the *beis midrash*, and asked him, "Father, did you speak with my father-in-law?"

"Didn't I write to you?" Rabbi Sofer replied briefly.

"And what did you write me?"

Rabbi Sofer stood up from his chair in anger. "What do you want?" he exclaimed angrily. "That I should get up from my chair this minute and have you sit here?"

The onlookers were shocked. Everyone knew that Rabbi Sofer chose his words carefully and said nothing without intent.

Rabbi Avraham Shmuel stepped backward, disconcerted. He now understood what Rabbi Sofer had meant in his letter. The post that his father had said that he would soon be getting would be the rabbinate of Pressburg. Rabbi Sofer had predicted his own imminent death.

Rabbi Sofer mentioned in one of his writings his hope that

the *Mashiach* would come by the year 5600 (1839-40). Perhaps he was expressing his awareness that he himself would not live past that year.

Rabbi Sofer expressed his strong belief that the *Mashiach* could appear at any moment.

"Regarding the coming of the *Mashiach ben David*," he wrote, "I will declare the following. Moshe was the first redeemer. But until the age of eighty, he didn't know or feel himself to be the redeemer of Israel. Even when G-d told him, 'Go, for I will send you to Pharoh,' he did not want to accept this mission.

"The same will apply to the final redeemer.

"On the day that the Beis Hamikdash was destroyed, a man was born whose righteousness made him fit to be the redeemer. When the time comes, G-d will reveal this to him and send him, and then this man will receive the spirit of the *Mashiach*. This is similar to the story of Saul. After he was anointed, a spirit of rulership and holiness came upon him that he had not previously felt.

"This is what happened with the first redeemer, and it also will be true of the final redeemer. That *tzaddik* himself will not know that he is the potential *Mashiach*.

"Due to our many sins, many have died, and we have still not merited that the spirit of the *Mashiach* should rest on them. Although they were fit, the generation was not fit.

"But one day, G-d willing, G-d will reveal His spirit to this man as He did to Moshe at the burning bush. G-d will send the final redeemer either to the Jews alone or to a king such as Pharoh, demanding, 'Let my people go.'"

The somber mood of *Elul* that year led into the awesome days of *Rosh Hashanah* of 5600 (1839). From *Rosh Hashanah* to *Yom Kippur*, the Jews of Pressburg spent ten days in awe and repentance in the presence of the Almighty.

Four days later, still in that sanctified atmosphere, the

Jews began their dancing and rejoicing on the festival of *Sukkos*.

Although an elderly man, Rabbi Sofer still retained his youthful strength. He told one of his sons, "I have the strength to go on living for another thirty years." When he dressed or took off his shoes, he did not have to lean against a wall, but stood on one foot.

But the joy of that *Sukkos* was marred by dark presentiments and sorrow.

At the very beginning of *Sukkos*, Rabbi Sofer was overtaken by suffering. But he strengthened himself and entered the holiday with joy.

The next morning, Rabbi Avraham Shmuel's four-year-old daughter Seril awoke crying hysterically.

Rabbi Avraham Shmuel came quickly to her bedside and asked the little girl, "Why are you crying, my dear?"

But she only continued sobbing inconsolably. Rabbi Avraham Shmuel held her against him. "Shh, my child, it's all right. You were only having a bad dream."

But Seril continued crying, and refused to say a word.

"Please, dear Seril," her father begged her. "Tell me what you dreamed."

Only after much pleading did Seril calm down and tell her father what she had dreamed. "In my dream, I was so sad and frightened because I thought that Grandfather had passed away."

"He is all right, Seril," her father assured her. "Don't let a dream frighten you."

That day, Rabbi Sofer sat at the *sukkah* surrounded by his family as was his custom, his face shining with joy. But his son Rabbi Avraham Shmuel sat at his right side with a sad look on his face.

"Rabbi Avraham Shmuel," someone at the table asked, "why are you looking so upset?"

Rabbi Sofer answered for him, "He is sitting here like a bridegroom among the mourners."

Everyone was shocked at this strange answer, and the joy of the holiday immediately dissipated. If they were all mourners, who were they mourning for? And why would Rabbi Avraham Shmuel be like a bridegroom? There seemed only one answer: when Rabbi Sofer passed away, they would all be mourners, and his son would have reason to rejoice like a bridegroom, for he would be the next chief rabbi.

Dark signs continued to occur. In the large synagogue, Rabbi Sofer was given the honor of lifting up the Torah scroll. As Rabbi Sofer held it up, the scroll ripped into two halves along one of its seams. Rabbi Sofer's face turned completely white.

At one of the meals in the *sukkah*, Rabbi Sofer wanted to give nuts and sweets to the children, as he did every year. But he had none to give. Every year, he told his servant before *Sukkos* to buy them. This year, for the first time in his life, he had forgotten.

Rabbi Sofer was extremely upset. His daughter, Simche, tried to calm him down. "It's all right, Father, it's such a little thing."

"Yes, but I am not used to forgetting."

But Rabbi Sofer said no more about his concerns. It was *Sukkos*, and he did not want anyone to worry.

And still he retained his great strength. After someone had obtained the nuts, Rabbi Sofer sat in his *sukkah* surrounded by his family, handing nuts out to his children and grandchildren. "What is the matter, child?" he asked one of the children.

"I can't open it," the boy cried.

"Give it to me." Rabbi Sofer took the nut between two fingers and casually cracked it open.

Hoshanna Rabbah came, and Rabbi Sofer stayed up in the *sukkah* with a number of friends until three in the morning. He was overcome by illness, and he lay down with terrible pains.

Still, Rabbi Sofer got up early the next morning to go to the synagogue. He put on his thallus and *tefillin* and began the prayers. But in the midst of *pesukei dezimra*, he was overcome by terrible pains, and he was forced to cut short his prayers.

As he walked home, his attendant comforted him, "Do not worry, Rabbi Sofer. The pains will soon pass."

"You are mistaken," Rabbi Sofer replied. "The gates of compassion have been closed."

They continued walking. "I feel like a general who has won all his battles," Rabbi Sofer said. "But when he came to one small, final battle, he lost—so what were all his other victories worth? Here also, I passed through *Rosh Hashanah* and *Yom Kippur*, but now I have fallen on *Hoshanna Rabbah*."

They continued in silence, and then Rabbi Sofer spoke again. "At a gathering, when a poor person starts crying and begging, he is tolerated. But when the celebration begins, the door is shut in his face."

Rabbi Sofer entered his room. He was never again to leave. That same day, he paid all his servants the money he owed them.

Rabbi Sofer's condition grew progressively worse. Doctors were called, and they declared that his life was in danger.

People flocked to the synagogues and poured their souls out praying for Rabbi Sofer and pledging charity in his merit.

Rabbi Daniel Prossnitz stood up before the congregation in the large synagogue and told the people as he wept, "*Rabbosai*, be aware whom you are praying for: a G-dly man, the leader of our generation, a man who has no equal in the entire world in Torah, wisdom and righteousness."

When the people heard these heartbreaking words, they burst into loud sobs.

261

Rabbi Daniel Prossnitz performed a *pidyon nefesh* for Rabbi Sofer's sake.

After this, an announcement was made in the name of the *beis din* that everyone should go home and eat his *Shemini Atzeres* meal without diminishing the joy of the holiday. But no one had the spirit to sit joyfully.

Despite his great pain, Rabbi Sofer adhered to his usual schedule for *Shemini Atzeres*. He requested a group of scholars to study a certain topic in Torah, on which he gave a talk. Someone asked him if he wished to be given a new name, but he replied, "No, there is still a good deal of time."

The next day, on *Simchas Torah*, Rabbi Sofer prayed in his room with a *minyan*. As was the custom, he was honored to be *Chassan Torah*, and he pledged eighteen liters of lamp oil.

After the prayers, he asked, "Why haven't my sons and daughters come to me for my blessing?"

Immediately his children were called for. When they came to him, he blessed them with joy shining on his face. "I must ask you to forgive me," he said, "for I have forgotten to go over the *parshah* twice and once in the *Targum*." He then did so. After this, he taught some original Torah thoughts.

During all this time, the attending doctors were astonished at how Rabbi Sofer could continue to act with such a clear mind in the midst of his suffering. They declared that this went beyond nature.

On the day following *Simchas Torah*, the doctors treated Rabbi Sofer with a catheter, and this offered him some relief. He said that an announcement should be made that his situation had improved, but that people should not cease praying for him.

Soon afterwards, however, Rabbi Sofer's optimism was dashed. An expert doctor from Vienna arrived. After examining Rabbi Sofer, he stepped out of the room and gave his prognosis. "I am afraid that the rabbi is very ill. I do not think that he will live longer than another day or two."

The terrible news spread throughout the city. No one went home. Everyone remained in the synagogues, pleading to G-d to save the life of Pressburg's holy leader.

Rabbi Sofer summoned Rabbi Avraham Shmuel and asked him to call all the *yeshivah* students.

When Rabbi Sofer's students were before him, he said, "If I mistreated any of you, I ask you now to forgive me."

Rabbi Avraham Shmuel burst into tears. "Father, my father," he exclaimed. "Perhaps it is my sins that have caused you to grow ill."

Everyone's heart was torn, and the students all began sobbing.

The community leaders met and drafted a letter to Rabbi Sofer. The letter stated that since Rabbi Sofer was now elderly and not in good health, he should appoint Rabbi Avraham Shmuel as his assistant to teach in the *yeshivah* and to render *halachic* decisions, bringing only the especially difficult questions to Rabbi Sofer. In addition, after Rabbi Sofer would pass away, his son would take his place.

The letter was written down by Rabbi Sofer's student Rabbi Mendel Hakohein and sent to Rabbi Sofer.

When Rabbi Sofer read this letter, he rejoiced and called out his thanks to G-d. "Call in my son, Avraham Shmuel," he told his servant.

When Rabbi Avraham Shmuel entered, his father asked him, "My son, do you agree to take my place?"

Rabbi Avraham Shmuel began weeping.

"Why are you crying, my son? Come to me, and I will bless you before my death."

Rabbi Avraham Shmuel approached his father and bowed his head. Rabbi Sofer lay his hands upon his son's head. Later, Rabbi Avraham Shmuel would tell that his father's hands burned like fire.

Rabbi Sofer recited a very long blessing, quoting the blessings mentioned in all of *Tanach* regarding leadership. The other people in the room looked on in silent awe at the sight of the aged rabbi, in the midst of his suffering, able to clearly remember all these verses. Rabbi Sofer finished his blessing, "May your grandfather Akiva be at your right side; your grandfather Rabbi Shmuel at your left side; an angel over your head; and I, your father, behind you. And I will help you."

Rabbi Sofer's other sons then came in, and he blessed them as well. In his blessing for his son, Rabbi Shimon, he quoted the phrase in the *Gemara*, "this one has based his teaching on the Torah verse," *Hai tanna akra ka'ee*. Many years later, when Rabbi Shimon became Chief Rabbi of Cracow, it became apparent that his father had been prophetically referring to this.

Then Rabbi Sofer requested that a *pidyon nefesh* be carried out in the *beis midrash* of the *yeshivah* downstairs, so that he could hear it and he could pray along with everyone else. He instructed the people to recite Psalms 57, 58, 59 and 75, and then to add the prayers at the end of the Psalms for a woman who is having trouble giving birth. Rabbi Daniel Prossnitz brought a hen for an atonement, according to the custom. But when Rabbi Sofer was handed a *siddur* to say the accompanying prayer, he immediately realized that through some error, the words, "This is my atonement" were missing.

At this ceremony, Rabbi Sofer's name was changed.

People then streamed to the cemetery to pray for him at the gravesites of *tzaddikim*, and all the synagogues were filled, day and night.

Soon afterwards, someone brought a document to Rabbi Sofer. The members of the community had donated years of their lives to him, asking G-d to subtract their years of life and transfer them to Rabbi Sofer. Altogether, the document stated, they had pledged twenty years of life for his sake.

Rabbi Sofer then made out a short will, dealing with his inheritance.

Meanwhile, the *chevrah kaddisha* came to Rabbi Sofer's bed. For the most part, he lay motionless, and they believed that his end was near. When he lay still, his hat was pulled down over his face so that no one could look at him.

When people began praying for him in the house, Rabbi Sofer grew upset. He told his son, Rabbi Shimon, "I don't know what these people want from me. Tell them to go home. There is still much time, and tomorrow we will pray with a *minyan*." Then he added, "The time has come for me to review all that I have learned, and they are disturbing me."

As Rabbi Sofer's sons sat before him crying, he turned to them and said, "Why are you crying? Fortunate is the person who spent his life as I did. Fortunate is the person who came into this world and acquired learning."

At another point, he told a Torah scholar, "For sixty years, I didn't let one day go by without learning and teaching, with the exception of *Tishah b'Av*. Even on the evening of *Yom Kippur*, I taught the service of *Yom Kippur*."

A while after this, Rabbi Sofer turned to those in the room and said, "Tomorrow morning at seven-thirty, the time will come."

Rabbi Sofer summoned the members of the *beis din* and the heads of the community.

When they came before him, Rabbi Sofer blessed them. He quoted the verse, "And this is the blessing with which Moshe blessed the people of Israel before his death."

"Don't we know," Rabbi Sofer asked, "that this was before his death? Obviously, we do. So what is the verse coming to teach us? It would have been right that Moshe bless each Jew individually, or at least tribe by tribe. But since this was before his death, he didn't have the time, and so he was forced to make do with one general blessing.

"The same goes for you, members of my community. I should have blessed each one of you individually, because you supported me and my *yeshivah* students so well. But I do not have the time. May G-d bless you a thousand times over."

Group after group of people entered the room, and Rabbi Sofer repeated this talk to them.

"I am consoled," Rabbi Sofer mentioned, "for we learn that *tzaddikim* die of intestinal diseases, and this is my illness."

Rabbi Sofer was insistent that his clothes and body be clean.

Early the next morning, a Thursday, Rabbi Sofer's bed linen and clothes were changed.

Rabbi Sofer put on his *tallis* and *tefillin* and prayed with a *minyan*. After the reading of the Torah, during the blessing, Rabbi Sofer felt his eyesight fading. He took off his *tefillin* and put on the *tefillin* of Rabbeinu Tam. He then prayed "*Uvah Letzion*—And a redeemer will come to Zion."

He took off his *tefillin* and gave them to his servant. "You have been a faithful servant. Take these for yourself. I no longer need them, for by tomorrow, I will be free of the obligation of *mitzvos*."

He asked for something to eat, and the doctors said that he should be given a light snack. It contained fruit, and he wasn't sure what blessing to make over it. He decided to make a general blessing. He tasted it, and declared that it had revived him. He then made an after-blessing.

Rabbi Sofer's student, the great Rabbi Menachem Prossnitz, entered and spoke with him. But soon, Rabbi Sofer told him, "Please leave the room now. My time to leave is drawing close." Rabbi Menachem Prossnitz left the room, and Rabbi Sofer requested, "I would like scholars to sit at the table next to my bed and learn, so that my soul will leave this world in the midst of Torah learning."

As the scholars sat and learned Torah, Rabbi Sofer stretched his hands out under the bed cover. He closed his eyes and squeezed his fingers, and his lips didn't stop moving.

Then he cried out loudly, "*Shema Yisrael*—Hear O Israel, the L-rd our G-d, the L-rd is One!"

When the hundreds of people who were gathered in the street and courtyard heard this, they answered with a mighty roar, "*Shema Yisrael*—Hear O Israel, the L-rd our G-d, the L-rd is One!"

Again, Rabbi Sofer cried out, "Hear O Israel, the L-rd our G-d, the L-rd is One!"

Again, the great crowd called out with all its soul, "Hear O Israel, the L-rd our G-d, the L-rd is One!"

Rabbi Sofer spoke the verse again. But this time, his voice could barely be made out. On Thursday morning at seven-thirty, on the twenty-fifth of *Tishrei*, 5600, his holy soul left this world.

"For our many sins, our leader is dead!" the *gabbaim* cried out, going through the streets. "The stores are to remain closed!"

Before Rabbi Sofer was buried, all the members of the community signed a document making Rabbi Avraham Shmuel the new Chief Rabbi of Pressburg.

At the time, Rabbi Avraham Shmuel was only twenty-four years old.

Rabbi Sofer had the right to appoint his son to be his successor. Still, the community also had the right to test the son to see whether he was fit for the post. Some people were concerned with Rabbi Avraham Shmuel's youthful age and wanted to consider the matter only after the funeral was over.

However, in the atmosphere that ruled then, there was a great push to accept Rabbi Avraham Shmuel immediately. Who at this moment was prepared to contradict Rabbi Sofer? A statement was drawn up appointing Rabbi Avraham Shmuel, and only those community leaders who signed it were given permission to approach Rabbi Sofer's coffin to ask his forgiveness.

As a result, this document was unanimously signed.

Rabbi Sofer had once signed a community decree that corpses had to be ritually cleansed in a special building on the cemetery grounds. But now the people wanted to perform this ritual cleansing on Rabbi Sofer in the *beis midrash*.

In the meantime, they were searching for a place to bury him next to the other previous rabbis of the city, but no place could be found. It would not be right to put off his burial until the next day or to store his body in the building in the cemetary. Some people decided to carry his body out of the city. This too was not quite respectful.

But as soon as Rabbi Sofer's body was carried into the street, people came from the cemetary and announced that they had found a burial spot for him.

Then people saw that this delay had occurred so that Rabbi Sofer would not be cleansed in the *beis midrash* in opposition to the decree that he himself had signed.

Rabbi Sofer's coffin was made of the table at which he had prepared his *yeshivah* lectures.

It was already afternoon, and it was clear that the funeral would last into the night. Torches were prepared to provide light for the funeral procession.

The massive funeral procession began. Rabbi Sofer's students walked before his bier, carrying the more than ninety volumes of his manuscripts.

At the funeral, in the light of the flickering torches, Rabbi Daniel Prossnitz gave the first eulogy. In the midst of his talk, he said, "How is it that the prayers of the men of Nineveh were answered, yet our prayer was not answered? This is because once the era of Rabbi Avraham Shmuel began, Rabbi Sofer's era ended. I now accept Rabbi Avraham Shmuel's authority. He is my rabbi and teacher. Even though he is still young, I am sure that he is a great light." Rabbi Prossnitz turned to Rabbi Avraham Shmuel and exclaimed, "You are our rabbi. *Mazel tov.*"

The thousands of mourners standing in the deepening twilight called out in a rolling murmur, "*Mazel tov!*"

The funeral orations continued long into the night. The vast crowd stood under the black sky, their faces lit only by the tall, flickering torches.

All the subsequent speakers who eulogized Rabbi Sofer also declared their allegiance to his son as the new Chief Rabbi of Pressburg.

Finally, Rabbi Avraham Shmuel eulogized his father.

In the week of mourning that followed, two or three Torah scholars eulogized Rabbi Sofer every day, arousing the people to realize the greatness of their loss.

Rabbi Sofer had been one of the most prolific Torah authors of his time. He left behind him voluminous Torah writings on most of the Talmud; writings on *Aggadah*; *chiddushim* on all four sections of the *Shulchan Aruch*; a commentary on the *Chumash*; a commentary on the five *Megillos*; a supercommentary on Ramban's commentary on the *Chumash*; his poetry; his diary of the siege of Pressburg (*Sefer Zikaron*); and his great collection of responsa, *Sheilos Uteshuvos Chasam Sofer*.

Rabbi Sofer left behind as well his children, who went on to become the Torah leaders of the following generations.

He left behind a network of students and adherents who spread his unwavering commitment to Torah throughout Europe.

He left behind a tradition and an approach to Torah that survived the fractures and upheavals of 150 years to continue to this day.

One of his students, Rabbi Zechariah Frenkel, wrote in a letter, "Even when he was alive, people said of him, 'He is holy, and from Moshe to Moshe, none has arisen like Moshe.'"

The Chasam Sofer was the scribe who wrote the words of longing for G-d and for Torah upon the hearts of hundreds of thousands of Jews. He impressed his seal of devotion to G-d on their hearts and arms, like a flame of fiery love that no water could quench. He was a soldier in the battle for Torah—not with a sword at his side, but in the words of *Yechezkel* (9:2), "with the quill of a scribe upon his belt."